Endorsements o
Finding God in Silicon Valley

Fame, fortune, and success are words that are synonymous with the best and brightest in Silicon Valley. In *Finding God in Silicon Valley,* Skip Vaccarello brings compelling stories of faith from some of the most successful leaders in the Valley that will truly inspire you. You will read how these leaders have gone from success to significance and found true meaning and purpose in their lives. For those curious about faith, I highly recommend that you read *Finding God in Silicon Valley*. It could change your life!

~ **Brent Jones, former SF 49er and Managing Director, Northgate Capital**

Watching Skip do his work is viewing Silicon Valley culture to the core. Have a conviction, take a stand, gather facts, obtain feedback, and then build, build, build. Writing is how Skip builds. His output is called *Finding God in Silicon Valley,* but his life is about finding people in Silicon Valley who have faith as a key element of their life. In *Finding God in Silicon Valley,* you will meet some great folks of faith.

~ **Kevin Compton, Founder, Radar Partners, a venture capital firm**

Skip Vaccarello has a passion for Silicon Valley, and a passion for God, and a deeply-rooted hunger to find the presence of the sacred in the work of creativity and innovation. If the finding of gold in this area was a game-changer 150 years ago, the finding of God in this area has even greater potential for impact. Skip has been doing spiritual detective work, and the results are inspiring and encouraging. Read it, and you may even find faith growing in yourself.
~ **John Ortberg, Author, and Senior Pastor, Menlo Park Presbyterian Church**

This book will move you and allow you to see God making incredible plays in Silicon Valley through His grace!
~ **Ronnie Lott, former All-Pro SF 49er**

Genuine integrity is the seamless integration of faith, family, and profession into a God-honoring life message. Skip Vaccarello gives us amazing life stories from kings of high-tech for whom God was the "secret sauce" leading them to true success in the midst of high-flying tech booms and, in some cases, from the depths of pain. This is a must read for business leaders and beyond—soak it in, learn, and be inspired!
~ **Bob Dees, Major General, U.S. Army, Retired**

Some people can be winning in one, two, or three aspects of their lives, but to have a truly balanced and successful life requires a strong foundation… a foundation of faith. Skip's

book reveals the "real stories" behind successful Silicon Valley entrepreneurs and leaders... what makes them tick and how putting their faith first has positively impacted their business, relationships, and their lives. If you are looking for inspiration and finding out what it takes to live a truly purpose-driven life, this book and these stories could change your life forever.
~ **Tom Tognoli, CEO, Intero Real Estate, a Berkshire Hathaway affiliate**

These stories breathe humanity, wisdom, ethics, and even joy into a technological age in search of truth. A treasure of insight into what matters, and why.
~ **Kelly Monroe Kullberg, *Finding God at Harvard*, The Veritas Forum**

Skip has skillfully woven together the captivating stories of influential men and women of the Silicon Valley, a place where you might not expect to find such vibrant followers of Christ. This is an encouraging read that I will be recommending to all my friends and people in my ministry. The message of Christ is alive and well and manifests in the lives of some of the most successful, influential, intelligent people in the world.
~ **Chuck Bryant, CEO and Board Chair, Pinnacle Forum America, Inc.**

Silicon Valley entrepreneurs are the epitome of the new economy, mixing innovative technology, new business models, and risk taking that is envied around the world. Hard science is generally accepted as the only truth in the Valley; what cannot be proven by a formula or physical demonstration is discarded as folly. Further, entrepreneurs from around the globe pilgrimage to the Valley's technology stage to compete against the world's best; self-confidence reigns even though many of their peers have previously failed. And these pilgrims bring their own core values, belief system and religion. It is against this crosscurrent backdrop that Skip Vaccarello has uncovered remarkable personal journeys in faith. While Silicon Valley Christians rarely use megaphones about their beliefs, their global contributions are significant and, rest assured, this book's stories are about dedicated individuals who struggle with life's challenges but have found that their fundamental belief in the Bible's foundation is their only enduring and true guiding light.
~ **David Lane, Founding Managing Director, Diamondhead Ventures**

There is nothing more powerful than telling a "story." Within the stories of these Silicon Valley global entrepreneurs and thought leaders are authentic experiences of God that withstand negative stereotypes, test the mind, and open one's heart to the exciting and improbable—a real encounter with God!
~ **Pastor Hurmon Hamilton, New Beginnings Community Church**

What's the point of Skip Vaccarello's new book and ongoing blog? To remind us that God is near and ready to be found by those who are seeking Him, even in one of the most competitive, egocentric, and hard-driving business climates in the world. The common assumption that there is no place for God in Silicon Valley is turned upside down by the remarkable stories of talented men and women who have discovered the centrality and relevance of faith in the San Francisco Bay Area. *Finding God in Silicon Valley* prompts us to ask an important question: How can I find God in my own circumstances?

~ **Mary Schaller, President, Q Place**

Finding God in Silicon Valley

Spiritual Journeys in a High-Tech World

Skip Vaccarello

Finding God in SILICON VALLEY

www.FindingGodInSiliconValley.com

Creative Team Publishing
San Diego

Softcover Edition

ISBN: 978-0-9963719-2-6

PUBLISHED BY CREATIVE TEAM PUBLISHING
www.CreativeTeamPublishing.com
San Diego

Printed in the United States of America

Finding God in Silicon Valley

Spiritual Journeys in a High-Tech World

Skip Vaccarello

Table of Contents

*****

*****

Dedication

I dedicate this book to the special people who have provided guidance and inspiration along my spiritual journey—to my parents, Vin and Lil, who gave me the foundation of faith; to my wife, Jackie, who is taking the journey of faith with me; and to my daughters, Julia and Christina, who are committed followers of Christ, and continue to inspire me with their faith.

Finally, I dedicate this book to my grandchildren, who are precious gifts from God—may they come to know and trust in Christ.

Foreword
Pat Gelsinger
CEO VMware

When I was asked to accept the role of CEO of VMware I was excited by the opportunity to take on my first CEO assignment. Doing so for an infrastructure software company like VMware was a great career progression for me, leveraging my background and doing so in a company that was in the middle of many of the key trends in the industry, like software-defined cloud and mobile computing. Further, moving to the Silicon Valley for the second time was exhilarating since Silicon Valley was, and I believe will continue to be, the center of technology and innovation, not just in the nation, but in the world. I was coming back to the hot bed of technology and in a big new job visible throughout the industry.

However, when my wife, Linda, and I had moved out of the Bay Area almost 25 years ago in 1990, we had no intention of "coming back." We wanted to raise our family in a different locale that was more family and Christian-values oriented. In fact, Linda had made a vow she was never coming back.

Thus, returning to Silicon Valley was a radical statement for Linda and me as a couple. It wasn't just for the job, but we were certain that God had something much bigger in mind. We were certain that this wasn't a new job but a platform for larger impact well beyond my day job as CEO.

We quickly found that God was working up stream with many parallel efforts to develop a new spiritual awakening in the Bay Area. Out of this have emerged several efforts like Transforming the Bay with Christ (www.tbc.city) that is beginning to unite the Christian community across the entire Silicon Valley.

My dear friend, Skip Vaccarello, asked me to speak at the Silicon Valley Prayer Breakfast that he chairs. The room was packed and vibrant. All of a sudden, long-isolated mega churches and parachurches were working together in newfound ways. Startups were anxious to achieve social and community impact, not just the billion dollar payout.

Were we living and working somewhere in the Bible Belt or in the tech-centric, scientific atheistic Silicon Valley? God was up to something, and we were finding ourselves in the middle of His plans.

Whether atheist, agnostic, Hindu, Muslim, Christian, or other, God is a central question that all of us with true intellectual honesty can't quite get around. In this book, you'll read stories of intellectual, innovative leaders who are finding critical impact in their lives from a relationship with a vibrant God. You will read how God has transformed the lives of these people by reaching down, miraculously intervening and changing them with dramatic and eternal implications.

Skip is a fellow traveler in this early journey, seeing a newfound social and spiritual awakening in the Bay Area. In the most unlikely of places on earth today, God is alive and at work. Skip and I are awed by what is going on. Every once in a while it feels like we need to be pinched to be certain this is really happening in this place.

In a thought-provoking manner, Skip provides a collection of amazing stories of leaders who have found God in Silicon Valley. Who would have thought in what externally might be considered as one of the most influential but anti-God places on earth, you'd hear of the vibrant, life-changing impact of God?

In a subtle and encouraging way, Skip offers these stories to help you consider your spiritual journey. Whether you live in San Francisco, Scottsdale, Salt Lake City, Scandinavia, or Shanghai, I hope you'll take a sojourn of thought and reflection as you consider with us the truths you'll discover in *Finding God in Silicon Valley*.

God and Silicon Valley: The Journey Begins

The greatest thing in this world is not so much where we stand as in what direction we are moving.[1]
~ Johann Wolfgang von Goethe

God and Silicon Valley! The two don't seem to fit, do they?

Tucked up against the rolling coastal foothills of Northern California, Silicon Valley is a hotbed of startups and thriving tech businesses with venture capital companies flocking to invest. It is the global center of technology where innovation and entrepreneurship flourish, and where fortunes are made. Venture capitalists and technology wizards form the perfect marriage of limitless money and bountiful creativity. Together they start companies like Google, Apple, and Facebook that change the way people work and live. Innovation, technology, and wealth are idolized. Self-sufficiency, self-centeredness, and pursuit of success reign.

Although there is no clear geographical area which defines Silicon Valley,[2] traditionally Santa Clara County, including the cities of Mountain View, Sunnyvale, and Palo Alto, form its heart.

Over the years, high-tech companies have popped up north, south, east, and west of those cities. Recently, San Francisco has become part of the tech boom, not only with companies opening in the city, but many young workers living and commuting south to work at high-tech firms. Far more than a grouping of Bay Area cities, "Silicon Valley is not a location. It is a mindset," says LinkedIn co-founder Reid Hoffman.[3]

The blog *Entrepreneurial Insights* reinforces this message: "Silicon Valley embodies more than a place with specific climates, latitude, and longitude. It is a mindset—a state of mind that places high value on innovation, on collaboration and competition, on failures and continued experimenttation."[4]

Silicon Valley's beautiful weather, entrepreneurial infrastructure, and seemingly relaxed atmosphere draw people. But the culture is hardly laidback. People work hard—sometimes 50, 60, and 70 hours per week to meet development deadlines, release innovative products, and drive sales. Salaries are high in Silicon Valley. The median household income in Santa Clara County, for example, is over $90,000 versus $53,000 in the U.S. as a whole.[5]

But Silicon Valley is an expensive place to live.

The City of Los Altos in Santa Clara County, population approximately 30,000, tops the list of the priciest four-bedroom, two-bath houses in the U.S. at nearly $2 million. Compare that to the average U.S. house value of $217,000. Eight of the ten cities and towns with the most expensive housing prices are in the San Francisco Bay Area.[6]

Although a fortunate few get rich quickly as stock options mature, many Silicon Valley residents work hard simply to make ends meet. For young millionaires, technology workers pursuing their dreams of riches, and service workers supporting the area's infrastructure, there is barely time for serious relationships, vacations, and leisurely home-cooked meals with friends and family.

So where does God fit in?

To a great extent He doesn't. The George Barna Group, a highly regarded research firm on cultural and religious trends, indicates in a 2013 study of people in the greater San Francisco-Oakland-San Jose area that the percentage of what it called "Highly Christianized" people is 58% lower than people in the U.S. at large, and church attendance is 30% lower.[7]

Steve Clifford, senior pastor of Westgate Church in San Jose, acknowledges that Silicon Valley is a hard place to do church. "Unfortunately, we are better known for what we are against, than what we are for… Any church starts out in Silicon Valley at a deficit. We are held in suspect."

John Ortberg, author of several books and senior pastor of Menlo Park Presbyterian Church (MPPC), notes: "This area is made up of smart skeptics." Silicon Valley is a stimulating and intellectual culture. Many are alumni of fine universities like Stanford and the University of California, Berkeley. "At the same time," Ortberg adds, "many of the highly educated have not considered Christianity, while others grew up as Christians but walked away from the church."

What Does "Christian" Mean?

According to Gallop, 77% of Americans identify themselves as Christian.[8] But what does it mean to be a Christian? "Christian" means different things to different people. Does Christian simply mean accepting that Jesus lived on the earth and was a great teacher worth emulating? Does it mean someone who attends church, either frequently or only occasionally? Does it mean accepting that Jesus is the Son of God, and that He was crucified and resurrected? Or does identifying as a Christian mean something more?

When asked about the underlying beliefs of his church, a pastor at a new members meeting responded "We major in the majors, not the minors." By the majors, he meant things that are clear in the Bible and that are basic to Christian faith. A list of majors of a committed follower of Christ means believing that Jesus is divine and the Son of God, that He died for our sins and was resurrected, that we are saved by grace, not by what we do, that the Bible is the Word of God, and that God is a trinity of Father, Son and the Holy Spirit. There is more than that, but those are the basics.

Being a Christian means accepting God's gift of grace, [9] putting our trust in Him as our Savior. Trust develops when we take the time to build a personal relationship with Christ.

The Silicon Valley lifestyle can leave residents busy, financially stretched, and skeptical, with little time or interest in God. But that is not the whole story. God is penetrating hard-hearted souls in Silicon Valley.

I am one example.

I was far from God when I came to Silicon Valley in 1979 to join a start-up. If asked, I would have said that I believed in God. If pressed, I would have called myself a Christian. But I had little sense of God and certainly did not practice faith. I did not attend church, did not read the Bible, and didn't even know the basic tenets of the Christian faith. I even thought that religious people were a little weird. Faith was of little concern for me. I had recently married and was embarking on a new career in an exciting new industry. Business, family, and staying in good physical shape were my priorities.

But I did find God in Silicon Valley. God wasn't an innovative technology, wealth, a big house, or success. He was Jesus Christ, the living Son of God, who we read about in the Bible. I describe my journey to faith in more detail in the chapter *Hollow Success.*

As a leader of technology companies for 35 years, I have had a front-row seat in Silicon Valley. I have participated in the revolution in personal computing in the 1980s, the growth in networking and communications in the early 1990s, the explosion in Internet usage in the late 1990s and 2000s, and the recent growth in social networking. Not only have I worked at companies involved in these areas, I have also had the opportunity to get to know Silicon Valley leaders engaged in these businesses who are also passionate followers of Christ.

This book is about how God is working in the lives of people in Silicon Valley—entrepreneurs, leaders of major companies, innovators in non-profit start-ups, scientists, and technologists.

Why is any of this important?

It is important because the way Silicon Valley goes, so goes the world. As the world's innovation leader for nearly a half century, Silicon Valley transforms the way people think, work, and live.

Could Silicon Valley be at the early stages of a spiritual revival? Possibly. There is evidence pointing in that direction.

Pastors like Clifford, Ortberg, and many others attract thousands of worshippers every Sunday. I count more than a dozen churches in the Bay Area with 1,500 or more worshippers each week. Church planters like bestselling author and pastor, Francis Chan, have come to the Bay Area. An organization called Transforming the Bay with Christ (TBC), formed by VMWare CEO Pat Gelsinger, plans to facilitate the planting of over 1,000 churches in the Bay Area before 2024.

Longtime CEO Tom Steipp says, "I see thousands of points of light rather than a single bonfire—churches, para-church organizations, and businessmen and women all working in different areas, but all seeking God's will and doing his work." Dave Lomas, entrepreneurial pastor of Reality Church in San Francisco—a church that in only five years has grown to 1,500 weekly attendees, most of whom are under 35 years old—comments that a minister friend told him that he has not seen such a movement of God in his 17 years of pastoring in San Francisco. New churches are opening, Christian entrepreneurs are building their companies to glorify God, prominent Silicon Valley business executives and venture capitalists put their faith at the center of their work. God is transforming lives.

Although it is sociologically interesting to consider the possibility of a Christian revival in Silicon Valley, it is more important to consider the lessons each of us can learn as we examine the lives and spiritual journeys of Silicon Valley leaders. How did they get beyond the trappings of financial and business success to find God? How did they overcome personal struggle and even tragedy to come to know Christ? How did they reconcile faith and reason and the compatibility of faith and science? And how did they discover meaning, purpose, and a calling for their lives?

In Matthew 19:26 in the Bible, when Jesus was asked by the rich ruler how he could gain eternal life, Jesus answered, "...with God all things are possible." God is doing the seemingly impossible in Silicon Valley—changing the hearts and attitudes of the rich and successful, and those desperately pursuing riches, power, and prestige. Having a tradition of disrupting the status quo with technology, Silicon Valley may be poised to challenge its perception as a wasteland of faith as well.

This book is about people finding God in an unlikely place, at an unlikely time, and in unlikely ways. God seems to work that way. The book is about God's transformative power—how He changes the lives of people who are open to His presence and gets the attention of those who are not.

In this book, I have grouped the Silicon Valley leaders' journeys of faith thematically into four sections: Faith and Success; Reason, Science, and Faith; Struggle, Adversity, and Faith; and A Higher Calling. In the final chapter, Concluding

Thoughts, I provide ideas and suggestions for you, the reader, to consider.

It is my hope that no matter where you are on your spiritual journey, you will consider the transformative power of God as displayed in the stories in this book—how He disrupts our intellectual assumptions, offers new meaning to success, turns tragedy into a blessing, and gives us meaning, purpose, and often a new calling.

Everyone I know has questions about God and faith—long-time followers of Christ, agnostics, and even atheists. We often gain insight when we hear people's stories. We can argue about philosophy and theology, but cannot argue with someone's experience.

In putting together this book, I interviewed over 80 Silicon Valley leaders. Their names were not changed and their permission was given for inclusion in this book. Some people I interviewed were reluctant to have their stories published because they didn't want to draw attention to themselves. They agreed to do so when I pointed out that although the story is about them, it is far more about how God is working in them and through their lives.

Collectively, God's story is powerful. It is transformative. We gain insight into God's character—His desire for us to know Him, His help in times of trouble, His steadfast willingness to meet us where we are, and most importantly His love for us.

Enjoy the journeys of faith in this book and consider the potential power of God in your own life.

Section One: Faith and Success

Faith led to new purpose and direction in my life.[1]
~ Paul Ely
Former Hewlett-Packard Executive and
Board Member

In Silicon Valley, we are driven by success and celebrate those who achieve it. Many come from elite institutions like Stanford and Cal Berkeley where they are conditioned to succeed. Others come from Asia, Europe, and other parts of the world in pursuit of the American Dream.

In Silicon Valley, we lust after the next greatest technology and jealously admire the latest company that goes public, creating instant wealth. Our heroes are often those who have made it big in business and achieved financial success.

Success often requires talent, hard work, and dedication, necessitating a time commitment that leaves little room for self-contemplation, a grateful heart, or any search for God. When we find success we credit our abilities, our hard work, and our drive. Success is sometimes just a matter of good luck—being in the right place at the right time. Whether success comes from hard work or good fortune, the thought of a transcendent God is far from our thinking, and time spent exploring that possibility is deemed unwise. "I did it once and can do it again" is the attitude that success fosters. We confirm our sense of control and reinforce self-sufficiency.

But are we really in control? Henry David Thoreau once said, "Most men lead lives of quiet desperation…" In those quiet moments, God sometimes breaks through in amazing ways and begins the transformation process.

And what is success? Is it achieving financial independence, taking a company public, or leading the development of a technology that will change how people work, play, or interact? Perhaps success is simply earning a good living and raising a stable, loving family.

Career and financial success can blind us to God's presence. Success can be a barrier or an entry point to faith. Once we encounter Jesus, however, He has a way of changing our perception of success. In this section, you will read the stories of how God transformed the lives of Silicon Valley leaders who found God and are living out God's plan for their lives.

Chapter 1
Gratitude: Discovering God's Impact on Our Lives

Perhaps it takes a purer faith to praise God for unrealized blessings than for those we once enjoyed or those we enjoy now.[1]
~ A.W. Tozer

In a quiet, suburban Palo Alto neighborhood, behind a brown cedar-shingled house, sits a one-car wooden garage with double olive-green doors. The State of California has designated this unassuming location as the birthplace of Silicon Valley. The garage stands behind the house where Dave Packard and his wife once lived, and where Packard and his colleague and fellow Stanford-educated engineer, Bill Hewlett, started Hewlett-Packard in 1938. Hewlett for a period lived in a shed next to the garage. The two friends tossed a coin to determine whether the company would be called Packard-Hewlett or Hewlett-Packard.

The first product to come out of Hewlett and Packard's workshop was an audio oscillator, an electronic device that generates electrical signals in the frequency of the range of human hearing. Their first large order came from The Walt Disney Company for their production of the animated film, *Fantasia*.[2]

From its simple beginnings, it is staggering to view the influence HP has had on technology and Silicon Valley. In the 1990s, a chart circulated that showed dozens of companies that were birthed or led by HP alumni. Although HP may have lost some of its glamour to Google, Facebook, Twitter and others as a leading edge technology company, it has endured and succeeded for decades before these companies were born. HP ranks number two behind Apple in sales,[3] and rightly deserves its reputation among the top Silicon Valley companies.

Through the mid-1970s, HP was primarily an instrument and test and measurement company; microwave devices, oscilloscopes, and medical equipment were HP's early products. The company introduced its first business computer—the HP 3000—in 1971 as it tried to make inroads in a competitive market dominated by IBM. But it floundered. The HP 3000 was plagued by performance problems soon after it was marketed. Unlike the way Hewlett and Packard wanted the company to run—with high integrity—HP's Computer Division started selling the HP 3000 before it was ready.

Dave Packard called on Paul Ely, a proven executive in HP's Microwave Division, to take over the Computer Division "to straighten out the situation."[4] Ely did just that. Within months, the problems were resolved, customer complaints decreased, and orders picked up. Although it took several years before HP fully established itself as a leading player in the computer business, Paul Ely was a key reason for HP's success.

Paul Ely built his entire career defying conventional wisdom, questioning accepted assumptions and the ways things were done. Paul's style, which was epitomized by the phrase "ready, fire, aim," was well suited for the fast-moving computer business. He opted for taking action quickly, evaluating the results, and adapting the accepted strategy if necessary. Paul uses a metaphor to describe this style of management: "It's like the British inventing tracer bullets during the Second World War. They were firing at moving targets, and when things changed quickly, they needed to fire and then aim. That is like the computer business."

Paul also defied conventional wisdom in his spiritual journey. By the time people reach their 70s, most have made up their minds on what to believe about God. Like many successful people, Paul Ely had forged his own road in business, following his instincts and playing by his rules. But at the age of 76, a sudden and unexpected revelation from God in a dream caused him to seriously investigate the evidence for the existence and identity of God, ending in his full acceptance of Jesus Christ as his Savior nine months later.

Gratitude underlies Paul Ely's journey to faith. Let's first set the stage.

Paul Ely's Background

I had heard of Paul Ely from my days in the computer business but had never met him until I interviewed him at his condominium in an upmarket senior-living center close to the posh Stanford Shopping Center.

Paul had achieved his Silicon Valley dream—wealth, prestige, and commercial success—by the time we met. I was meeting with him not so much to talk about his Silicon Valley business success, but to hear firsthand his extraordinary journey to faith.

Tom Steipp, an HP manager who worked several levels below Paul, is a follower of Christ. Tom said this about Paul: "I suspect that many of my colleagues at HP were surprised when they heard about Paul's conversion. I don't think that any of us ever thought that Paul Ely would submit to anyone's authority, except his own. On the other hand, when that conversion finally occurred, Paul did what he always does; he put all his energy into knowing and serving the Lord."

Before interviewing Paul, I read his memoir, *Ready, Fire, Aim,* which came out in 2013. The book describes his upbringing, career, and faith story. I looked forward to meeting Paul.

At 82 years old, I was struck by Paul's apparent fitness and sharp wit. He is handsome, with black-gray hair and warm brown eyes. As he spoke, I sensed his commanding leadership style, reminiscent of a military officer. As we sat down together in his home office, Paul immediately put me at ease with his warmth as he shared his story.

"Even though I attended church as a child with my parents, faith never resonated with me. As I got older, I stopped attending church. I gave little consideration to religious beliefs or practice in college and in my career. Although I would have said I believed in God and was a Christian, faith never penetrated my thinking. I was not interested. I was born to be an engineer. That is where my interest was."

As a child, Paul loved math and science and was fascinated by mechanical and electrical things. His dad, an engineer, had a major influence on his son—building various devices with him, sharing his lessons with him, and challenging Paul's thinking and opinions in extended dinner conversations. His dad also taught him not to accept the status quo, and to question people's opinions and assumptions. "Throughout my career," says Paul, "all my good ideas and successes came when I refused to accept when people said, 'It can't be done.'"

Paul's career started at Sperry, an engineering and defense contractor, where he worked as an engineer for nine years. In 1962, he was recruited to join Hewlett-Packard, performing research using microwave wavelengths to identify gaseous compounds. Paul took to HP's open style of management and the so-called "HP Way" of doing business. The HP Way had been defined by Bill Hewlett and David Packard in the early days of the company. It emphasized integrity, bold leadership, opportunism, and a decentralized leadership style that encouraged innovation by people at all levels in the company.

HP was also known for its generous benefits, including tuition reimbursement which Ely took advantage of. He earned his Master's degree from Stanford in engineering.

Paul rapidly advanced to upper management positions, often questioning the status quo along the way. He challenged the process by which products were developed and tested and was able to improve the cycle time from development to product introduction. Hewlett and Packard emphasized the "walking around" style of management and, as a result, got to know Paul. They were impressed by Paul's work ethic, attitude, and ability to get things done. For these reasons they were comfortable having him take over HP's troubled Computer Division in 1973.

Paul's success in turning around the Computer Division led to an appointment as an HP Vice President in 1977. In 1980, Paul was elected Executive Vice President, a member of the executive committee, and a member of HP's Board of Directors. At the age of 48, Ely was at the pinnacle of his career.

Ready, Fire, Aim

The phrase "ready, fire, aim" stayed with Paul throughout his career at HP and served him well. His promotion required that he move to corporate headquarters in an office close to HP's CEO, John Young, Paul's direct manager for many years and a person Paul greatly respected. His new role required Paul to engage in corporate activities unrelated to the computer business. As an operational person by nature, Paul grew frustrated with his new role. He grew more frustrated by some of Young's decisions.

One was the decision to allocate resources to HP's minicomputer business at the expense of HP's personal computer (PC) business. Paul and others in the PC division wanted to innovate by developing a PC with a graphical user interface to compete with IBM's PC. Instead, Young decided to have HP simply develop a clone of the IBM PC.

What was most frustrating to Paul, however, was Young's implementation of a consensus style of management that required the buy-in of people at many levels before a decision was made. Consensus management contrasted with Paul's "ready, fire, aim" approach, and, in Paul's opinion, was not an effective way to run a company in the rapidly changing computer business. Paul's frustration led to his parting HP after 23 years at the company.

Although Paul's career advanced after his departure from HP with a stint as CEO of Convergent Technology, and eight years in venture capital, among other positions, he now admits that he regrets his decision to leave HP. "My lessons in humility and patience had just begun. Had I remained at HP in my new position that training would have intensified and continued. I longed to stay at HP but my pride and ego were in control."[5]

His time after HP was marked with personal struggle. In 1987, his wife, Barbara, was diagnosed with Alzheimer's disease. Paul spent much of this period after HP caring for her. She died in early 2000.

God Gets Ely's Attention

In all the years expanding his career and achieving business success, Paul had a singular focus. Faith wasn't a part of the equation.

But in a distinct moment, all that changed. Paul says, "I never gave serious consideration to God; that is, until the morning of April 15, 2008." In an instant, God got Paul's attention in a dream. Paul saw how his loving parents had cared for him as a child in spite of the difficulties they experienced during the Great Depression. He relived his undergraduate days in college, both the friendships he enjoyed and the intensity of his engineering studies. He saw his first date with Barbara, their marriage, and the births of their two sons. He saw his whole life play before him, including his business success.

"As I lay there, quite suddenly an overwhelming feeling of intense gratitude and thankfulness for the good fortune that had filled my life swept over me. The intensity and depth of the experience are well beyond my limited ability to describe or relate. It continued as I saw my entire life flashing before me like a YouTube video."[6]

Paul realized that God had been working in his life all along. "It wasn't my great skill, it wasn't my 'ready, fire, aim' approach, and it wasn't my education. It was God who had provided all my good fortune."

At the end of his revelation, Paul heard the message, "Paul, you must find God."[8] For the first time, Paul realized that God was present and active in his life. He understood that God was behind his success.

Gratitude — A Biblical Perspective

The Bible says, "Every good and perfect gift is from above."[7] Gratitude—acknowledging God's care—is a basic tenant of the Christian faith. It starts with thanking God for sending His Son, Jesus, as a sacrifice to die for our sins so that we can be saved.

The key verse is John 3:16, "For God so loved the world that he gave his one and only Son, that whoever believes in him, shall not perish, but have eternal life."

But who was this God? "God was a puzzle to me," says Paul. "I suspected there was a God out there some place, but that was the extent of my understanding."[9]

Paul's started on an intense nine-month journey to find God.

He began his search for God by finding a church. One Sunday he wandered into Menlo Park Presbyterian Church (MPPC) where he was immediately moved by the music and by the sermon delivered by the church's senior pastor, John Ortberg, a renowned preacher and author. Paul began attending MPPC weekly.

A notice in the church bulletin announcing a prayer class caught his attention. Not only did he attend the class, but he was soon invited to attend a weekly men's Bible Study. Sixty to seventy men attended the study. "What was so amazing was the scriptural knowledge of the men in that room," says

Paul. "I felt God working in that room and redoubled my efforts to know and relate to Him."[10]

In addition to Bible reading for the weekly men's group, Paul began reading the Bible on his own. But without context, he struggled to understand God from the Bible alone. With a voracious appetite for knowledge of God, he consumed several books including *The Shack,* a bestseller at the time in which the Trinity is presented as an allegory, and *The Language of God* by Francis Collins.

In *The Language of God,* Francis Collins, an M.D. and PhD and accomplished geneticist who headed the genome project, describes his journey from atheism to Christian faith and reconciles science, particularly evolutionary biology, with faith. With a background in the sciences, Paul found *The Language of God* helpful in understanding the coexistence of science and faith.

In *The Language of God,* Collins references *Mere Christianity,* a Christian classic by C.S. Lewis. Paul devoured *Mere Christianity* and found it "captivating."

Of particular influence to Paul was *Loving Monday* by John Beckett. Paul's sister knew Beckett and gave this book to Paul at Christmas in 2008. Beckett, a committed Christian and MIT graduate, joined his father's manufacturing company and eventually took it over. In the book Beckett writes how work can be filled with meaning and purpose by integrating one's faith with work. Beckett ran his company based on biblical principles. The idea triggered Paul's recollection of how HP worked. Although Hewlett and

Packard had not been explicit about their faith, they developed a principled culture at the company.

God was transforming Paul's heart and mind. He was changing Paul's definition of what true "success" was and what a well-lived life looked like.

Paul noticed that on the inside back cover of *Loving Monday,* his sister had written a reference to John Beckett's website—www.LifesGreatestQuestion.com. In perusing the site, Paul read how Beckett came to faith and noticed Beckett's summary of the Christian Gospel which Paul found persuasive. The summary ended with a prayer:

> *Jesus, I need You. I repent for the life I've lived apart from You. Thank You for dying on the cross to take away the penalty for my sins. I believe You are God's Son and I now receive You as my Lord and Savior. I commit my life to follow You.*

With tears of gratitude, Paul prayed that prayer. In February 2009 at the age of 76, Paul, a Silicon Valley icon who had ignored God most of his life, found the God he was searching for—the God who died for him and the God who was behind his life and good fortune.

A Transformed Life and the Work of the Holy Spirit

Finding God was not the end of Paul's story. Paul's conversion transformed his life. "Faith," he says, "led to new purpose and direction in my life. I wanted an authentic relationship with God, wanted to know the Bible." He wanted to "be like the other Christian men I met and admired." Paul doubled down on his spiritual journey by joining a second and a third Bible Study and fellowship groups.

At the age of 83, Paul Ely's life is different. His goals and desires have changed. "I want others to know the joy that comes from knowing Jesus, just as I did after I accepted Him." God, through His Son, Jesus, and the work of The Holy Spirit, changed Paul's life to conform to God's design for him.

It is my experience that people who turn to faith, especially those who do so later in life, want to share with others the joy that comes with knowing God. New believers suddenly realize what they were missing in life and want others to know.

Paul talks with delight how many in his family, including his sons and grandchildren, were moved by his example to embark on their own search for God, ending with their acceptance of Christ as their Savior.

The Holy Spirit

The lives of people change when they commit to faith in Jesus Christ. Christian scholars would refer to this as "the work of the Holy Spirit" – the third Person in the Holy Trinity.

In John 16:7, Jesus tells His disciples that after He is gone, He will send the Holy Spirit to them. The Holy Spirit is the quiet voice that praying and listening Christians hear to guide them to live and act according to God's will. The Holy Spirit enters the lives of people when they receive Christ as their Savior. By listening and obeying the Holy Spirit, peoples' lives change over time.

Paul wrote his memoir and agreed to my interview and inclusion of his story in this book in the hope that others will consider faith. In addition, Paul channels his desire to help others find God by volunteering part-time with Global Media Outreach (GMO), an Internet-based ministry that helps people with questions about Jesus. According to GMO, one billion people visited the GMO website to find out more about Jesus. (www.GlobalMediaOutreach.com)

Paul is living his days in gratitude for all God has provided, and is working to help others find the joy he is experiencing. The amazing changes in the later years of his life show how God is creative in finding people and drawing them to Him. He can use our greatest tragedy and our most dramatic successes to reveal Himself, and can do so at any stage of life—even after we retire. He can and will use different people in our life—a neighbor, a co-worker, or even a family member—to pray for us and show us who He is.

Paul's second wife, Geri Cherem, a committed Christian who had been Paul's administrative assistant since 1968, had been praying for Paul for years. On that April morning in 2008 when Paul told Geri about his revelation, Geri said with a smile, "I had been expecting something like this to happen; now it has."

Chapter 2
Success and Surrender

Christ says, "Give me All. I don't want so much of your time and so much of your money and so much of your work: I want You..."[1]

~ C.S. Lewis

We celebrate self-reliance in America. Self-help books often top the bestseller lists. Descriptions like "rugged individualism" and "self-made man," and phrases like "pull yourself up by the bootstraps" and "find the greatness within you" echo throughout our history and culture. We learn that success and achievement are up to us. We admire those who achieve success through determination and hard work. Silicon Valley is known for its insane work ethic and people who have made something out of themselves. But self-reliance can lead to the character flaws of self-centeredness and self-absorption, as it did for Dr. John Dearborn.

John Dearborn is a well-known surgeon in Silicon Valley. Nearly everyone I know who has had joint replacement surgery had it done by John Dearborn. Not only is he a popular orthopedic surgeon, but he is a person of faith who prays with his patients before surgery. When I reached out to John to interview him for this book, he humbly responded, "I'd be happy to talk with you, not because I have it all figured out, but if anything God has taught me would be an encouragement to others, I am in." I discovered in my interview with Dr. Dearborn that God intervened in his life in a big way—turning a highly successful but self-centered man into a humble person who surrendered his life and successful practice to God.

John Dearborn's office is located in Menlo Park, a fashionable community close to Palo Alto and Stanford. His office had a new, fresh look to it. It was smartly lighted and decorated. As I looked more closely, I noticed Christian literature among the magazines, and pictures with biblical themes on the walls. Clearly, this was unusual for any office in Silicon Valley.

As I sat in his private office across from him, I could not help but notice that he is a striking man—handsome, fit, and friendly. He told me about his family background, schooling, professional work, and how he came to faith. I was struck at how remarkable a man he is. He was candid but humble about his success, and he was open about his shortcomings, his faith, and his reliance on God. "My identity," he remarked, "is as a disciple of Christ, who has saved me in spite of my many faults."

John Dearborn is a Silicon Valley success story. He had a string of achievements under his belt even before he began his practice as a surgeon—high school valedictorian, water polo All-American, Stanford graduate, and University of California, San Francisco medical school graduate. His accomplishments grew as he experienced professional success as an orthopedic surgeon. He cofounded the Dearborn-Sah Institute for Joint Restoration in Menlo Park. He and his partner, Alexander Sah, perform their surgery at Washington Hospital in Fremont, California. In July 2013, *Consumer Reports* recognized the Dearborn-Sah Institute at Washington Hospital as one of the top five highest rated hip replacement programs in the country.[2]

John and his partner perform over 1,500 joint replacement surgeries each year, a significant increase from the 70 replacements each year performed before John started his practice there. He is revered in his profession and is often asked to present at medical conferences and write articles for prestigious medical journals.

John's rise to success as one of the top orthopedic surgeons in the country is remarkable but his story is not without struggle, particularly in his personal life

A Self-Absorbed Life

John Dearborn is a confident man. In accomplishing so much, he lived a life of self-reliance and self-centeredness. "The self-focused life," he notes, "quickly becomes a self-absorbed one which is a very lonely place. There's little room for others, certainly no room for God. In fact, in that world, the self-centered individual says, 'I am God.' The choices I made revolved around me as did the things I valued—image, comfort, wealth, power, and prestige."

John admits to drinking and to having self-centered relationships with women throughout high school and college. "I was not living a moral life, mostly around parties and alcohol. I was living pretty much on the pleasure principle, not reigned in." As John recalled his earlier life, he was overcome with emotion. Clearly, now as a follower of Christ, the regret of his past behavior is still raw in his mind.

Although he attended church through high school and on rare occasions in college, he never absorbed the messages. "The seed that was being sowed in me was basically falling on rocky soil. In college, I ran pretty wild until I realized that my behavior might prevent me from achieving my professional goals."

Finding God

Early in medical school, God got John's attention. John was invited by a master's swim coach to attend a Bible study. He comments, "God drew me out of the life I was living. I was confronted with the fact that I was a sinner. I questioned my salvation, sought out a new level of accountability, and even briefly broke up with my fiancé to establish purity in our relationship." God was beginning to transform John's life—going from self-centered, to reliance on God.

For most new believers, this takes time; it does not happen in an instant. As our relationship grows with Christ, we also come to know the gap between the life we are living and the life Christ would have us live.

Two years later, John and his wife, Danielle, began to attend a small church in San Francisco and a faith-based small group. "This group was foundational to my faith," says John. For the first time, he had a faith community. "Beside me in the living room were several people equally broken, pursuing a right relationship with God. God began to show me that He is faithful and wanted to be Lord of all areas of my life." God began to soften John's self-centeredness. He admits, however, that he was slow to release his grip on some of the idols he still had, especially that of self-image.

It took two major health issues to get John Dearborn's complete attention. In 2006, he was diagnosed with a herniated thoracic disk which compressed his spinal cord and progressively numbed his legs. "I felt powerless and terrified." John turned to prayer. He says, "I could not restore the sensation to my legs and could not live life the way I wanted. I felt truly reliant on God for the first time in my life. I spent the next several months surrendering my life to the Lord every morning before my feet hit the floor, counting on Him to give me strength through the day." In time John recovered his ability to walk, but he has had to cut back on high impact activities.

Three years later, in 2009, he received another reminder of his dependence on God. He started having severe incidents of atrial fibrillation (AFIB)—an erratic heartbeat. The first incident occurred as he was driving across the Dumbarton Bridge, a 1.6-mile span that crosses San Francisco Bay. "I wasn't certain I would make it to the other side, but somehow I did." As the AFIB incidents recurred over the next several months, John's prayer life and time with God took on greater importance. "During one prayer time, I heard God saying that I had not yet fully surrendered to Him."

Surgery cured his atrial fibrillation. More importantly, John fully surrendered to God. "My idol of self-reliance was replaced with a clear understanding that I am a beloved child of God. There is nothing I can do to change the way He feels about me. I don't need to worry about image management. I know God loves me no matter what I do. Despite all the things we do, all our rebellion, God still loves us. Who wouldn't want to follow a God like that?"

John Dearborn had lived an enviable life—high school valedictorian, top student at Stanford, and a top surgeon with a successful practice. His success, however, led to a self-centered life. God convicted him of his sinful self-centeredness, and he became a follower of Christ. But it took physical setbacks for John to fully surrender his life to Christ.

Surrender

"Surrender" is not a popular word in America, especially in Silicon Valley. Surrender means giving up on something—implicitly something important in which we are heavily invested. Countries shamefully surrender in war. Companies reluctantly surrender a market leadership position to a better competitor. Sports teams surrender titles to stronger opponents.

Surrendering our will to God is scary business. We work hard to make our way in the world. We invest time, energy, and money in our education, career, and physical well-being. Most people—especially high achievers in Silicon Valley—like to think of themselves as powerful, not weak; self-sufficient, not dependent; in control, not subservient. When we experience success, it is particularly difficult to give up our will. Success seems to prove that our way is the right way.

Success, however, can also have its costs: an inflated ego, controlling behavior, and broken relationships due to the time and energy invested to achieve success. The Apostle Paul in 1 Timothy calls the undeterred pursuit of success in the form of riches self-defeating: "Those who want to get rich fall into temptation and a trap and into many foolish and harmful desires that plunge people into ruin and destruction. For the love of money is a root of all kinds of evil."[3]

We should note that the Apostle Paul says that it is not money, but the *love of money* that constitutes the trap.

God in His infinite wisdom gives us free will. We can choose to live a life following our will and desires without any consideration for the transcendent. Money, power, prestige—in a word, *success*—can easily become our idols. Or, we can surrender our will to the purposes God intends for us.

It often takes a crisis for us to surrender our will to God. "This happens because we tend to be unresponsive to God's gentler nudge," writes Oswald Chambers.[4] A crisis presents us with a crossroad. We can push forward acting on our own strength and will, or we can submit to God's will. Physical ailments drove Dr. John Dearborn to the feet of God and the total surrender of his idols to God.

From a Christian perspective, an idol is anything we worship other than God—fame, power, money, etc.—and that becomes the focus of our lives.

A person surrendering to God is someone who gives priority to what God wants. It means seeking God's desires for us though prayer, Bible reading, meditation, and listening to the wisdom of other believers. It means living by God's moral standards as expressed in the Bible. It means loving our neighbors as ourselves. It means seeking God's guidance in how we live day to day—what job we take and how to perform that job, who we are to marry and how to behave in that marriage, and how we allocate our resources: money, possessions, and time. It means living a life of integrity and generosity.

Surrender is what God requires of those who are his followers, including those in Silicon Valley. Jesus said in Luke 9:23: "If any man would come after me, let him deny himself and take up His cross daily and follow me." *The Message* paraphrase of that biblical passage reads, "Anyone who intends to come with me has to let me lead. You're not in the driver's seat—I am."

Surrender is not easy. Every day, followers of Christ fail to live up to the life Christ would have them live. This apparent hypocrisy turns off skeptics to Christian faith. But the committed follower of Christ knows he is susceptible to wrongdoing (i.e., sin) in God's eyes, falling short of God's design for us. The committed believer repents—meaning turns away—from the offenses against God, loved ones, and others, knowing that there is forgiveness with Christ. He seeks forgiveness from God and those he wronged and renews his effort not to repeat the offense.

I struggled with surrender for years after I became a follower of Christ. I was a high achiever and competitive, with a will to succeed. I mistakenly thought that surrender meant giving up on achievement and success. Later I discovered that God does not want us to surrender our desire to succeed. He wants us to succeed with a desire to honor Him in the process, with Him at the center, giving Him our full attention. God wants us to trust Him and rely on Him. Our motivation to succeed is not for self-aggrandizement, but to honor and glorify God.

The first sentence of the first chapter in Rick Warren's bestselling book, *The Purpose Driven Life*, is telling: "It's not about you." Warren goes on to say that our purpose in life is far greater than our personal fulfillment, peace of mind, or happiness. "You are born," he says "*by* His purpose and *for* His purpose." Life does not make sense unless we understand that.[5]

I understood that as a child of God, the object of my work and success was not to satisfy my ego, but to please God. The Bible verse Colossians 3:23 permeated my attitude about work: "Whatever you do, work at it with all your heart, as working for the Lord, not for human masters…"

That changed not only my attitude, but how I went about my work and my life.

The good news for me, for Dr. John Dearborn, and for people whose stories are in this book, is that a life surrendered to God is filled with meaning and purpose. It is a life with a focus on living out God's intention.

Surrender to God does not necessarily mean that we forfeit success. Dr. John Dearborn's success as a top orthopedic surgeon continued after his commitment of faith. He admits that he may lose some business due to his transparency about faith, but he is fine with that. He remarks:

> *I think we should certainly count the cost before we make a commitment to follow Christ all the way because a decision like that will cost you your life. In exchange, and I am certain of this, you will receive the life God has planned for you from the beginning – the life designed for you knowing your gifts. So as a disciple of Jesus I feel like I have been called to go make disciples using the gifts God has given me and in the context in which he has placed me.*

Mike Griego

Like Dr. John Dearborn, Mike Griego, a hard-driving, successful Silicon Valley-based business executive, was challenged to reconcile the perceived conflict between surrender and success.

Born and raised in Southern California in a family that did not attend church, Mike began his Christian journey while in high school through encouragement from friends and leaders in a local church youth group. He graduated from Occidental College in Los Angeles, married, and moved to Bay Area to attend Stanford's Graduate School of Business where he earned an MBA degree. Prior to founding MXL Partners, Mike had a distinguished Silicon Valley career in sales and sales management with such companies as IBM, XL/Datacomp (StorageTek), the Gartner Group, and Intelliquest.

A pivotal incident in Mike Griego's faith journey happened at a meeting of Christian businessmen in the mid-1980s. A pastor who was leading the meeting asked Mike a question. "Mike, you sell IBM computer systems for the glory of God, right?" Although Mike had been a follower of Christ for many years, he was stunned by the question. He comments, "I was dumbfounded. I stared back blankly, not really knowing what he was talking about. In fact, I never thought of God when I was selling computers and was quite certain that God didn't care about my computer selling."

That question led Mike on a journey to understand what it meant to follow Christ and what it implied for one's work. As Mike studied the Bible and engaged other Christian business leaders in the discussion of faith and work, he came to understand that business is a calling; just as work in vocational Christian ministry is a calling. Even Jesus worked as a carpenter for most of his life, and the Apostle Paul worked as a tentmaker. Griego remarks, "…it isn't what one does as a profession that is important; it's who one is in their work and daily life… What matters is our devotion to the calling of God, to love Him and our fellow man, and to surrender our life, gifts and talents for His purposes."

His Faith Challenged

Following the business downturn in 2001, after 9/11, Griego says he felt "a holy nudge" to start his own business which he called MXL Partners. In spite of risky circumstances, including the need to provide support for his wife and three children entering college years, Griego felt God was compelling him to make the move. But getting business was tough. He reached the point where he was not sure he could continue and began to wonder if God had really compelled him to start the business. At a very low moment, he prayed for God to show him a sign that starting the business was what God wanted him to do. Within an hour he received two telephone calls for projects he could do immediately. Mike remarks, "I wept at my desk. I do believe I got my sign."

Mike sees his work as his ministry. He can influence many people globally not only with managing sales through his training and sales consulting business, but also by being an example of how a godly man works. In addition, he writes a weekly blog called Biblical Viewpoint[6] in which he offers a biblical perspective on various topics including faith and work.

God transformed Mike Griego's concept of work, resulting in his surrendering his work to God's intentions for him. Mike says that he's come full circle; he runs his business today "...for the glory of God—reflecting simply good work and services in the marketplace done with gifts and talents offered up for His purposes and direction."

Dr. John Dearborn embraced Christian faith after he recognized that his success led to a self-absorbed life that was contrary to God's intention for him. Mike Griego compartmentalized business success and faith until he was confronted by a simple question from a pastor. His faith took on a new depth when he was able to answer that question.

Pat Gelsinger came to Silicon Valley at the age of 18 to work as a technician at Intel. That was his first step in a career that led him to the top levels at Intel and EMC, and eventually to VMware, the fifth largest software company in the world where he leads the company as its CEO. With success, his faith, however, was just lukewarm; that is until God intervened. We will look at Pat's spiritual journey in the next chapter.

Chapter 3
Success Redefined

The foundation stones for a balanced success are honesty, character, integrity, faith, love and loyalty.[1]
~ Zig Ziglar

Pat Gelsinger is CEO of VMware—a hot Silicon Valley-based company specializing in cloud-based computing and the fifth largest software company in the world. Silicon Valley is far from the rolling hills and farm country where Pat Gelsinger grew up in Pennsylvania Dutch country. Pat's rise to the top echelon in high technology is nothing short of spectacular.

He was brought up as a farm boy. Both his mom's and dad's families were farmers. Although his dad was not a farmer, Pat worked on his uncle's farms and loved the work. Pat jokes that as a youth be became knowledgeable in cow chips, not computer chips.

In the late 1970s Pat took an interest in electronics, especially personal computers like Radio Shack's TRS-80 that he used while attending Berks Technical Vocational High School. In his junior year in high school, Pat won a scholarship to attend Lincoln Technical Institute where he earned an AA degree in 1979 at the age of 18. He completed his course requirements to graduate from high school in the same year.

With graduation approaching, Pat started looking for jobs. He applied to East Coast firms, including IBM, but was intrigued when a recruiter from Intel, a Silicon Valley-based semiconductor company, came to the Lincoln campus. Pat was hired and started at Intel as a technician in quality assurance. He quickly advanced in quality assurance and then to positions in chip design. While working full-time, he used Intel's college tuition reimbursement program to complete his BSEE (Bachelor of Science and Electrical Engineering) at Santa Clara and went on to Stanford where he earned a master's degree in electrical engineering and computer science.

At Intel, Pat worked on a variety of processors and was the architect and design manager on the 80486, which provided the processing power needed for the personal computer revolution through the 1980s into the 1990s. At age 31, Pat was appointed Vice President, the youngest person to hold that position at Intel. A few years later, he was named Intel's first Chief Technology Officer. Pat went on to attain leadership roles in almost every Intel processor through 2010.

Pat worked at Intel for 30 years both in Silicon Valley and Portland, Oregon. In 2010, he was recruited to work as the Chief Operating Officer at EMC, located in the Boston area. And in the fall of 2012 he came back to Silicon Valley to join VMware as its CEO.

Faith Background

Today Pat is a committed follower of Christ who readily admits that for the first 18 years of his life, he was not really a Christian.

Pat grew up in a church-going family. He attended church every Sunday. At the age of 14, he was voted president of his church's youth group. By all outward appearances, Pat was a shining example of a Christian young man.[2] But Pat's life out of church did not reflect biblical values. He experimented with what he calls "the temptations of our age"[3] and hung around guys who exhibited questionable behavior.

It wasn't until he came to Silicon Valley that his faith became real. He started attending Santa Clara Christian Church, a biblically based church, and participated in a small group Bible Study. Pat contrasts what he was learning at his new church with the church of his youth. He recalls that the church of his youth didn't emphasize teaching the gospel, didn't confront him with the need to develop a personal relationship with Christ, or the consequences of sin, or the convicting work of the Holy Spirit.[4] Pat came to realize that he was engaging in a lifestyle not consistent with biblical values.

In a sermon in February of 1980, his pastor, Gary Fraley, preached from Revelation 3:15-16: "I know your deeds, that you are neither cold nor hot. I wish you were either one or the other! So, because you are lukewarm—neither hot nor cold—I am about to spit you out of my mouth."

"I was challenged and convicted," says Pat. "I could clearly see that my other-six-days-of-the-week lifestyle placed me in a lukewarm category at best. I was as Revelation so boldly declared ready to be spit out of the mouth of the Lord."[5] Pat did not want to be "lukewarm." From that point forward, Pat was on fire for God and truly began his faith journey.

A Crisis of Faith

As is true for all followers of Christ, however, Pat's faith journey was not smooth. Shortly after committing to God, he had a crisis of faith. He was torn between continuing with his business career and going into full-time, vocational ministry. Just when he was at the point of deciding to take the path of vocational ministry, God set before him a Bible verse that changed his decision. The verse is Colossians 3:23:

> *Work willingly at whatever you do, as though you were working for the Lord rather than for people.*

Pat realized that his work could become his ministry. He decided to continue his career in business. As a business leader living out his faith every day, Pat had the opportunity both to deepen his faith as he confronted serious business issues, and to influence others positively. At the 2014 Silicon Valley Prayer Breakfast, Pat remarked, "At every phase of my career I've always said, 'Okay, now I'm in the next phase of my full-time ministry.' I like to think I have a congregation of 18,000 today as CEO of VMware. It's not Menlo Park Presbyterian Church or Reality Christian Church. It's VMware, and that's the church that God has given me to be a minister to, and be a steward."[6] Pat's desire to be a good steward of the business God gave him to run spilled over into his desire to be a godly husband and father as well.

Balancing Faith, Family, and Work

A challenge facing nearly every Silicon Valley business person and professional with whom I spoke is how to balance work, family, and faith. Silicon Valley is a demanding place to work and live. So how does one balance the needs of family and work and stay true to one's faith? Pat developed a set of guidelines which he described in his first book, *Balancing your Family, Faith & Work,* and expanded into a later book titled, *The Juggling Act: Bringing Balance to Faith, Family, and Work.*

Pat emphasizes the importance of having a personal mission statement. The mission statement comprises three elements:

- Mission — a succinct statement of who you want to be as a person
- Values - the principles by which you want to live, and
- Goals - what you want to accomplish.

Pat says, "If you haven't done the hard work of writing these things down, any path will get you there, because you don't know where you want to go."[7]

To the mission statement, Pat offers a way to prioritize one's use of time.

> 1. Prioritize God – "Create a unique relationship between yourself and God that is consistently reinforced by the way you use your time to remain in dialog and relationship with Him. Choose routine areas of your life to remind and encourage you. Have daily devotion time with God."
>
> 2. Prioritize Family – "Establish your family relationships in such a manner that other factors do not squeeze out that precious family time. Put clear boundaries in place and be prepared to make tradeoffs such as those between work and family that will be clear evidence of where your priorities truly reside."
>
> 3. Work Hard – "Be a great employee. Realize that you are not working for your boss, your president, or your company. Instead, you are working for God. Recognize that He is the singular source of your ultimate reward. Look past anything that might distract you from being a great employee."

It is not easy to keep one's priorities in balance. For balance and accountability, Pat emphasizes getting a mentor. One of his mentors for many years was Andy Grove, former CEO of Intel. Today he has two mentors with whom he regularly meets. And, as a way to give back, he mentors others.

God is at the center of Pat's life—a contrast from his days as a church-going youth when faith was little more than a label and something practiced on Sundays only.

Pat's faith directly influences how he is living his life. "As a born-again believer in Jesus Christ, my faith is at the foundation of who I am, what I stand for, what I dream of accomplishing, and what I desire to become as a man."

Pat Gelsinger is "on fire for God"—no longer lukewarm. For Pat, "on fire" affects not only the way he lives, but how he can make a difference.

Born Again

The term "born again" comes from John 3:6-7 in the Bible (NLT). Jesus says, "Humans can reproduce only human life, but the Holy Spirit gives birth to spiritual life. So don't be surprised when I say, 'You must be born again.'"

"Born again" means that once we accept Christ as our Savior we have a new life. The Holy Spirit enters our life and helps us to live differently. We live not for ourselves but to be more like Christ.

Transforming the Bay with Christ (TBC)

When Pat returned to Silicon Valley in 2012 to work at VMware, God put a vision on his heart to do something about the secular nature of Silicon Valley and the Bay Area, and to help heal the brokenness in the Valley. When Pat lived in Portland, he noticed the impact that compassion and service can have on a community. Churches in Portland put denominational differences aside to cooperate with city leaders, business professionals, and other community leaders to meet vital local needs.

With that vision in mind, he gathered a small group of his venture capital friends, business leaders, and prominent pastors to talk about how followers of Christ could have an impact in the Bay Area. The initial meetings included top venture capitalists Kevin Compton, formerly of Kleiner Perkins, and Promod Haque, of Norwest Ventures, as well as nationally known pastors who were leading churches in the Bay Area, including John Ortberg of Menlo Park Presbyterian Church, Chip Ingram of Venture Christian Church, and Francis Chan, renowned author and preacher.

In a talk at a TBC gathering in January 2015, Pat shared, "This area with all its wonderful things still experiences brokenness." He cited high crime rates, poor schools, and homelessness that are as bad as or worse than other areas in the country. It was out of this brokenness—economic, educational, and spiritual—that the idea for TBC was formed.

TBC has three primary areas of focus: unifying the Christian community in the Bay Area, amplifying the level of service by churches helping the disadvantaged, and multiplying the number of Bay Area churches. One of TBC's goals is to help start 1,000 new churches by 2024. To do so,

TBC hopes to support entrepreneurial pastors by building an ecosystem, much like those found in high-tech accelerators, to include experienced pastors and business people.

Being "on fire for God" means living for God at home, at work, and in the community. Being on fire for God means leading lives that show evidence of gratitude and Christian faith in the lives we live.

Pat Gelsinger is much more than a successful Silicon Valley business leader; Pat is a disciple of Christ. Success took on a new meaning for Pat Gelsinger, as it does for born again followers of Christ. Success means living as Christ would have us live—24 hours per day, 7 days a week. It means leading by serving.

Like Pat Gelsinger, Sanjay Poonen, a longtime Silicon Valley executive, looks at success differently than most other technology leaders. Like Pat, success means living as a disciple of Christ and leading by serving. But his story of faith is different than Pat's.

Sanjay Poonen

Sanjay Poonen has certainly experienced career success. Not only are there few Christians in senior ranks in corporate America, there are very few people from India who are Christian and very few senior Indian Christians in executive ranks today. Sanjay currently serves as an executive vice president at VMWare. Prior to VMware, he was president and corporate officer of technology and industry solutions at SAP, one of the largest software companies in the world. Sanjay also served in executive roles at large companies, including Symantec, Informatica, and AlphaBlox. He started his career as a software engineer at Apple and then Microsoft, and has two patents to his credit.

Sanjay also experienced educational success. Growing up in India, he was an exceptional student. He came to the U.S. to attend Dartmouth College on a foreign-student scholarship. At Dartmouth, Sanjay earned a BA, summa cum laude, in computer science and engineering. He went on to earn a master's degree in management science and engineering from Stanford, and an MBA from the Harvard Business School, where he was recognized as a Baker's Scholar, the top honor in the class.

Spiritually, Sanjay was born and raised in a Christian family in India. His dad, Zac Poonen, is well known as a prolific writer and teacher of the Bible and started over 60 churches in India and around the world that have over 6,000 members among them. Once on his own in college in the U.S., however, Sanjay admits that he was challenged spiritually to make faith his own, rather than merely that of his parents. "My interest in God faded away because I was enamored by the things of this world," says Sanjay. "But the roots of my home church, CFC India, and the Christian campus groups like Campus Crusade and Navigators helped me." In his formative 20s, Sanjay found he needed to enter the "eye of the needle" himself; he couldn't ride into the Kingdom on the coattails of his dad or his family roots!

As a long-time technology worker and executive, Sanjay acknowledges that it is not easy to live out one's faith in the workplace. In talks he gives to churches and community groups, he challenges his audiences of business people to "dare to be Daniels in the workplace." Daniel was an Old Testament Jew of great wisdom who found success in the Babylonian and Persian empires. Daniel was uncompromising in his religious convictions in the midst of persecution that once saw him thrown into a den of lions.

Sanjay challenges his audiences with questions like this: "Is it possible to be on fire for God in the workplace, or is that just for pastors? How do we deal with the fame and fortune that come from success in business? How do we deal with enemies in the workplace who are plotting against us? Is it possible for Christians to be honest all the time, no matter the circumstances? How do we balance work, family, and life?"

Personal Values as a Way to Success

Sanjay found it useful to crisply define his top ten values as a way to navigate businesses challenges with a Christian foundation. His decisions flow from these values.

1. Focus on eternity, not making decisions that violate biblical principles for short-term gain – "My life is a vapor. I am a citizen of heaven."
2. Work hard, with humility – "I'll work hard at everything I do. If the Lord grants me success, I'll fall on my knees in humility, praying for grace to be faithful."

3. Maintain godly behavior – "I will live boldly for Christ, keeping my Christian behavior excellent, so that others can glorify God."
4. Pray and listen for God's direction constantly – "I will be open to the direction of the Holy Spirit, wherever it might lead and whatever it leads me to speak and act."
5. Give generously – "I will be generous with the resources the Lord has given me."
6. Put ego aside – "I will do nothing out of selfish ambition."
7. Be a servant leader – "I will not seek my own glory. Instead, I will seek to honor God and encourage those around me."
8. Listen and be patient – "I will be careful with my words and actions."
9. Seek the input of mentors – "I will make the godly my heroes."
10. Embrace change – "I will be on fire for God, seeking to be a change agent, not satisfied with the status quo."

Clearly, these ten worthy values are a challenge to follow consistently. Sanjay says that he needs God's grace and the Holy Spirit to strengthen him in his journey of faith.

Success for Sanjay comes out of balancing his work life with family and actively serving in the community. He and his wife, Kathy, live in Los Altos with their three young children. He serves as an elder at his church, Abundant Life

Christian Fellowship, which is a diverse Bible-believing church, where people from a variety of ethnic groups worship.

"My titles, accomplishments, and degrees are not important when it comes to the kingdom of God," declares Sanjay. "I am humbled when Jesus said, 'The first will be last, and the last will be first.' The hierarchy and the way in which God's Kingdom works are the exact opposite of the ways in which the world works. That is why some of the people who have the most impact for the kingdom are folks who are the most humble and the least accomplished. It is fantastic that the Lord can also work through a CEO, but it's not because they're a CEO, it's hopefully because they have a humble heart to serve God.

"I have found that I often learn the most associating myself with those who are from the humblest walks of life. That is Servant Leadership. My goal is to live every day as if it were my last, all for the Glory of God, to whom I owe so much."

Pat Gelsinger and Sanjay Poonen reflect the values of other Silicon Valley leaders profiled in this book. Those values include hard work, integrity, humility, service, and generosity. Pat and Sanjay strive to succeed at work, but not at the expense of their families, or by compromising their faith and integrity. Their model is Jesus Christ. Success is to use their God-given skills to serve Christ and others, and to carry out Christ's purpose for them in their work, homes, and community.

Chapter 4
Hollow Success

God enters by a private door into every individual.[1]
~ Ralph Waldo Emerson

There is a sense that anything can happen in Silicon Valley. With hard work, one great idea can become a million-dollar company. Silicon Valley is the place where dreams come true, companies come to life, and today's failure may lead to tomorrow's great success. The sky is the limit. Many an innovator has seen their cutting edge idea bring notoriety as well as fortune. Adventure, success, and wealth are synonymous with Silicon Valley.

My wife, Jackie, and I were excited about the possibilities Silicon Valley offered when we moved from the East Coast to the Silicon Valley in 1979. In doing so, we had to leave behind friends and family and an area we both loved. I had lived my whole life in New England and Jackie much of hers.

My Upbringing

I was born in 1948 and grew up in Waltham, Massachusetts, a city of 55,000 people 10 miles west of Boston and made up primarily of second- and third-generation immigrant families—predominately Italian, Irish, and French Canadian. For a city of its size, Waltham was a surprisingly close-knit town. Many had relatives living in the city. Local politics and the love of local sports teams from Little League through high school were two threads that knit the city even closer together.

My parents moved to Waltham shortly after they were married, to live in a two-bedroom apartment owned by my dad's aunt. That is where I was born. We moved to a larger home when my mom was pregnant with my brother. Although large to us, it was a small home by today's standards— three bedrooms and one bath. My brother and I slept in the same bed, while my sisters shared another bedroom. It was a comfortable home and on a tree-lined, dead-end street that backed up to a playground. The playground had two baseball diamonds, a basketball court, fields for football, and a play area with seesaws and swings for children. I spent nearly every waking hour on that playground. My childhood revolved around sports—baseball in the spring and summer, football in the fall, and basketball in the winter.

I thrived on competition, and even made up games when the weather was bad. I played football in the snow and basketball in my basement. I made a hoop out of the ring of a coffee container, coated it with tin foil so we wouldn't cut our hands, nailed it to a rafter, and used a softball to play. When alone, I played baseball on my bed. I used baseball cards for the players, a pencil and marble for the bat and ball, and shoe boxes and books for the fences. The Red Sox won nearly every one of those games.

I was blessed with parents who loved and cared for me. They showed their love in many ways—coming to nearly all my games, taking an interest in whatever I was doing, and sacrificing to pay for family vacations.

My mom was Protestant; my dad was Catholic. Since my mom and dad were married by a Catholic priest in a Catholic church, my mom had to agree to raise her children in the Catholic Church. My neighborhood was predominately Catholic—Irish and Italian—with a few Jewish kids mixed in. The playground was abandoned on Wednesday afternoons as the Catholic kids were in "Sunday School" at our local church. My most distinct memories of those classes were how afraid I was of the nuns and how I struggled to memorize the Baltimore Catechism. I can still recite the beginning of the Catechism. "*Who made us?* God made us. *Who is God?* He is the Supreme Being, who made all things…" I had a real sense of God as a child but after high school, He seemed to fade away into my childhood memories.

In my senior year at Waltham High School, I was co-captain of the football team, which went undefeated and tied for the Class A championship in eastern Massachusetts. I was the co-winner of the Most Valuable Player award and won the league scoring title. Although I was small at 5′ 9″ and 160 pounds, some colleges recruited me to play football. The University of Connecticut offered me a full four-year scholarship, but I was intrigued by a vice president at Yale who suggested that if I take a year at Phillips Exeter Academy in New Hampshire and did well, I might be admitted to Yale. My parents, who earned only a modest income, encouraged me to apply to Exeter. They wanted the best for me, even if it meant more sacrifice for them. If I was admitted, I would, of course, be giving up a four-year scholarship to UConn.

I applied and was admitted to Exeter. It was a very tough year. The academics were rigorous but I performed well enough to interest top colleges including Harvard, where I decided to attend. My path was set. Looking back, I can see how God had His hand on me even then, although I thought I was getting in on my own merits.

All of the students at Exeter were required to attend a religious service of their choice on weekends. I chose the Catholic service since I grew up Catholic. Students were required to sign in to make sure we were credited with attending. If we did not attend, we could be put on restrictions of some sort. The most popular religious service was "Jew Cong"—Jewish congregation—that met on Friday nights. Although there were not many Jewish students on campus, this was by far the most popular service. My classmates preferred sleeping in on Sunday mornings and getting their religious attendance requirement out of the way on Friday nights since there were no girls at this all-boys school to date anyway.

The Catholic upbringing of my early years was giving way to a sense of feeling disconnected from faith and church. The services offered little meaning to me. Religion seemed to be about rules, which I often broke. I would go to confession and within hours, I sinned again. Rather than feeling consumed with guilt, I disengaged. It was only later in life that I realized that faith is not about adherence to rules—which are often man-made and not biblical—but about a relationship with Christ. The required worship attendance added to my growing disenchantment with organized religion. This was the beginning of a 20-year hiatus from the practice of faith.

When I entered Harvard in the fall of 1967, God was the last thing on my mind. My four years at Harvard were turbulent years on campus and in the country. Harvard students, like many other college students at the time, were ardently against the War in Vietnam. The draft made the issue personal for many, including me. During my time at Harvard, there was a riot in Harvard Square, university buildings were taken over, a student strike shut down classes, and business recruiters—especially those associated with the war effort—were blocked from coming on campus. The staid halls of Harvard were caught up in the protests as students wanted to bring attention to the university's support for the war effort and its perceived anti-women and racist policies. It was a season of change and discontent. Nathan Pusey, the Harvard President at the time, was quoted as calling my class—the class of 1971—"the worst class ever."

The turmoil of the early 70s deeply affected my classmates and me. Thirty-eight percent of my graduating class did not go to graduate school right after graduation.

Many of us "dropped out" and took non-traditional jobs for Harvard graduates—cab driver, farmer, bartender, and fisherman. Some did not work at all. It took us a while to find our bearings but within five years those stats had changed. A study taken five years after we graduated showed that 90% of our class had attended or were attending graduate schools.[2] It simply took time for my classmates and me to get our lives together after all the turbulence we experienced at college.

An Unusual Path to Silicon Valley

I graduated with a concentration in economics. Although I was attracted to business activities, I could not see myself working for a large company. Starting and running a small business interested me. After graduation, a couple of classmates and I started a waterbed business—my first start-up, if you can call it that. We were not particularly committed to the business, and it was not successful. We earned less than $2,000 and folded it within a couple of months.

After abandoning the waterbed business in the fall of 1971 and working at some part-time jobs to make money, I took a position at a nonprofit organization with a mission to help mentally handicapped adults and their families. I continued in that field with three different nonprofits for seven years, culminating in a two-year stint as the Executive Director of the newly formed nonprofit the Arthur J. Clark Workshop in Waltham. That was my second start-up.

In 1973, I began attending the Boston University School of Management on a part-time basis while working full time. I earned my MBA in 1977. It was a grind to work full time and attend graduate school part time. The best part of business school was that was where I met my future wife, Jackie. She was an attractive, intelligent Wellesley graduate. Although we were both dating other people at the time, we became friends over beer at the local bars after class. We hit it off immediately. We found it easy to talk with each other and shared similar values, especially about the importance of family and friends. Neither of us took ourselves too seriously. Although we sometimes had discussions on serious topics, we shared a sense of humor. We started dating exclusively in 1975 and married in 1978.

All the pieces of my life were falling into place. I had finished business school, was making a reasonable living, and married a wonderful woman.

Then opportunity came knocking. Just a year after getting married, the founders of a start-up company in personal computing software called Personal Software asked me to join them as they prepared to move the company from the Boston area to Silicon Valley. Even though my only exposure to software was an introductory programming course I took as an MBA student, I was fascinated by these new machines—the Commodore Pet, Radio Shack's TRS-80, and of course the Apple II. The games were fun to play—especially Microchess, which was developed by Peter Jennings, one of Personal Software's founders. What interested me more than the games, however, was a product in development—an electronic spreadsheet, later named VisiCalc. Up to that point the personal computer industry was small and dominated by engineering types. I could see that this electronic spreadsheet would open the world of personal computing to the masses. It provided a simple way to put together financial forecasts, personal budgets, and even bowling averages. I wanted in.

Dan Fylstra, an MIT and Harvard Business School graduate, was Personal Software's other founder. He spearheaded the effort to develop the spreadsheet with the spreadsheet's originators and developers, Dan Bricklin and Bob Frankston of Software Arts. I am not sure what Peter and Dan saw in me. Perhaps it was my interest and enthusiasm for their business and potential for VisiCalc. Perhaps they saw my leadership capabilities in running the nonprofit. Certainly, it was not my technical capabilities. Nevertheless, they asked me to join them as their first full-time employee. I was excited to do so, and to embark on a new career in an innovative industry.

Jackie was also ready for a new adventure. She had been working in a Boston bank and was not that enthusiastic about her boss. Having one of my sisters living in San Jose made the thought of making the transition to California easier for us. We would have family close by, we would have each other, and we would have a new start in an amazing new community.

In the spring of 1979, I started as the Vice President of Operations at Personal Software—later renamed VisiCorp. This was my third start-up. I was 31 when Jackie and I moved to Silicon Valley. It was an exhilarating time to work in the industry in its infancy. But Silicon Valley was different from Boston—not just the weather and landscape, but the culture.

Coming from Boston with its fanaticism about politics and sports, I was surprised by the lack of interest in either—especially politics. Cocktail talk was about high-tech companies poised to take advantage of the most recent innovations. The heroes were high-tech company executives, not the candidates for office. Yes, you could hear such discussion, but compared to what I had experienced in Boston, the contrast was dramatic.

The local Boston news was dominated by election, legislative, and political corruption news. In the Bay Area, news focused on local crime with barely a mention of political news. The *San Jose Mercury News* had an entire business section dedicated to high-tech news. Boston radio had multiple sports talk stations. The Bay Area had one.

In Silicon Valley at the time, people were quick to move from one company to the next to take a job at a company with the next greatest technology or with a path to going public. Unlike New England, the college you attended was less important than what you could do. The casual dress belied the intense work environment. People worked very hard and for long hours.

As with most start-ups, my job included doing a range of activities. I loved the challenge and the excitement to be part of something new. VisiCalc was introduced to the market in the fall of 1979 on the Apple II and became a hit, almost overnight. Steve Wozniak, Apple co-founder, attributed VisiCalc as one of the two factors—the other was the floppy disk—which accounted for the Apple II success.[3]

As the company grew, so did my responsibilities. Work consumed most of my time. I had to adapt from my 9-5 routine at the nonprofit to working 12 hours per day in this Silicon Valley start-up. Jackie took a position as a financial analyst at another Silicon Valley company. But there was a different, new adventure beckoning us: parenthood. In 1982, Jackie left the workforce and became a full-time mom when our first daughter, Julia, was born.

The next three years, from 1982 through 1985, were a period of transition. I took over as president of Communications Solutions, Inc. (CSI), a newly acquired subsidiary of VisiCorp, where I joined the founders of CSI in running this networking and communications company. In 1985, our second daughter, Christina, was born.

When we moved to Silicon Valley, Jackie and I had a meager net worth, most of which was in the equity of our home. By the mid-1980s, our net worth had dramatically increased. We had two beautiful daughters and owned a four-bedroom home in Los Altos, an upscale town located in the heart of Silicon Valley. Life was good. I had everything that a man could ever want. But somehow, I did not feel fulfilled. Something was missing.

"A God-Shaped Vacuum"

Even though I longed for success and appreciated the money I earned, I sensed that there was more to life than business, competition, and success. I didn't know what. What more could I possibly want in life—perhaps more money? It was the miracle of birth—especially the birth of our first child—that caused me to pause and think about God and life. "Who is this God? What role does He have in my life?" were thoughts I had. But the busyness of life—long hours at work and now helping to raise our children—caused those thoughts to fade in the background. Occasionally, in the quiet moments of life—just before going off to sleep or looking at a mountain range or a sunset—I would ponder who God was and what life was about. And while success and money were good, I was finding that they offered no long-term satisfaction.

There was a void in my life that I couldn't fill on my own. Centuries earlier, mathematician and philosopher Blaise Pascal identified the feeling I was experiencing as the realization that there is "a God-shaped vacuum" in each of us. I knew there had to be more to life. I needed God, but didn't know it. Success was good, but not all I thought it would be. What was I missing?

These thoughts were leading me down a path toward God. The rules of my childhood faith had been rejected long ago but here I was, a successful man in most people's eyes, and I was finding it wasn't enough. I needed to know if there was more. I asked, "Is God real? Is there evidence to prove that He did, in fact, exist?" I had come full circle. Did those catechism questions of my youth have the answers: *"Who made us? Who is God? ..."*

Little did I know that this was my new journey, my journey of finding out that there was a God who was real, a God who loved me and had a purpose for my life, a God who had opened doors of opportunity for me, a God who had blessed me and given me success, a God who led me to Silicon Valley, the center of free thinking and technology, and a God who showed me that He is real.

Although I sometimes thought about God, I did nothing to seek Him out, that is, until 1985 after the birth of Christina. She was born in July with a genetic condition that required close monitoring, necessitating blood tests every other day and then weekly. The stress for Jackie to bring Christina and three-year old Julia to the hospital to watch the nurses prick Christina's heel to draw a small tube of blood, left Jackie and the kids in tears.

The invitation to Julia by a friend to attend Vacation Bible School (VBS), as well as the offer to pick her up and take her home for the two-week program, was an immense relief to Jackie. She could focus on Christina's needs. I was comfortable with Julia attending VBS, as I had a positive experience in a VBS session as a child.

The timing of the invitation to VBS and the impact it had on our lives by bringing us into a church family, was an amazing example of God's grace that we didn't recognize at the time. Julia loved VBS and asked when she could return to the church. We did nothing about church, however, until later that summer when a neighbor invited Jackie to attend a church service—a weekend when I was on a business trip in Paris.

When I called home to see how Jackie and the children were doing. Much to my surprise, Jackie told me she went to church. "You did what?" I asked. She repeated that she went to church. I was astounded. She explained how much she enjoyed the peace she felt at church and how much Julia enjoyed Sunday School.

Soon Jackie began attending church on a fairly regular basis. At one point, I agreed to "try" church with her. Some of my reluctance in attending was because this was a Protestant church. Having grown up as a Catholic, I was not sure what to expect at this church. I was also aware of what I had been taught—that the Roman Catholic Church was the only true church. But the years of not attending any church softened my resistance. I felt surprisingly comfortable in this church. Although I do not remember the content of the sermon that Sunday, I do recall that Pastor Kent Mead's message aroused my curiosity about faith. And the people were friendly. They were not weird and, in fact, looked like other Silicon Valley people. I also noticed that the church had several families with young children.

A Decision for Christ

I began to attend with Jackie. As I did, Kent Meads' messages began resonating with me. His messages applied biblical principles to real-life situations to which I could relate. I was prompted to begin to read the Bible seriously. Up to that point, my only real exposure to the Bible were passages I had heard at the Catholic church I attended as a child and in a "Bible As Literature" course I had taken at Harvard. I also began researching the evidence for the Christian faith by reading various books, including some by Josh McDowell and C.S. Lewis. I took an adult Sunday School class on the Bible and asked many questions. The Old Testament prophesies that were fulfilled by Jesus, and the evidence for the resurrection were particularly convincing to me.

Over the next several months, I overcame most of my doubts—although I still had many questions—and accepted Christ as my Savior. I did not answer an altar call or anything like that. I simply accepted the truth of the Bible and vowed to learn more. The year was 1986. Jackie made a similar decision at roughly the same time. My decision was at first intellectual—it made sense by what I read and noticed in the world around me. When I have told this story, I would feel somewhat embarrassed. I did not have any immediate vision or emotional acceptance of Christ. But I realized years later that others, including C.S. Lewis, the renowned Christian intellectual and writer, had the similar experience of coming to faith first based on the evidence.

Over the next few years my faith deepened and became emotional as well as intellectual. I began to understand the admonition in 1 Thessalonians 5, to "...pray continually..." Much of my thought life during the day was about God. My life's focus became how I could serve Christ—at home, in the workplace, for the church, and in the community—and at the same time I developed a strong desire to help others know the joy that comes from having a personal relationship with Christ.

My career continued to advance following my conversion. We sold CSI three times to three different companies, the last time to 3Com in 1988, all at higher valuations. I stayed at 3Com for a year as a general manager before co-founding The Saratoga Group, a multimedia training company, with the two founders of CSI. This was my fourth start-up. In 2000, we sold that company to Channelwave Software, where I stayed for a year. I worked from 2001 into 2008 as a consultant and executive coach before taking the position as president and CEO of Applied Weather Technology, a company providing software and services for the maritime industry. I worked at AWT from 2008 through 2012.

Success—or, rather, the lack of lasting fulfillment that comes from success—led to faith in Christ for me. What was missing for me was God. Once I came to faith, I realized that a fulfilling life is not about a string of achievements, power, or wealth. Faith and a relationship with Christ gave me an eternal perspective that helped provide context for whatever success or failure I experienced. Contentment was the result. This was not contentment with the way things were in this challenging world, but contentment with who I am as a child of Christ and His purpose for me.

Success takes on a new meaning. It is not about business, financial, or athletic achievements. Success is about growing closer to Jesus, discovering God's purpose for my life, and living out the calling God has for me as a husband, a father, a friend, a businessman, and a member the church and community.

I sense that God has called me to help others in their spiritual journeys. I put God's calling into a personal mission statement that I first wrote in 2001.

My mission is this:

To be a blessing and to serve other people.
I hope to encourage, inspire, and lead people
to faith in Jesus Christ,
and hope to use the platforms God gives me
to accomplish my mission.

My mission leads me, among other things, to engage in one-on-one discussions with not-yet-believers who are interested in exploring questions about faith, to write this book, and to chair the Silicon Valley Prayer Breakfast, an event that highlights the personal stories of Silicon Valley and other leaders as a way to encourage those in attendance to consider faith.

I am also a founding partner at New Beginnings Community Church in Mountain View, California, an ethnically and culturally diverse Bible-believing church with a focus on serving the community and reaching those who are not yet followers of Christ.

Section Two: Reason, Science, and Faith

Faith is different from proof; the latter is human, the former is a Gift from God.[1]

~ Blaise Pascal

Silicon Valley companies rely on teams of intelligent workers with marketing, engineering, and science expertise to succeed. They determine what products to produce, how to design and develop them, and how to market those products. Reason and science skills are critical to developing ever more sophisticated high-tech products that sell. The business leaders and scientists whose stories I discuss in this section are followers of Christ. They use their intelligence in business and apply it to their faith. Faith and reason are compatible concepts they embrace, not adversarial ideas that some would have us believe.

It is important to recognize that faith is not confined to the spiritual world. We make acts of faith every day. When I step on a plane, I have faith it will take me safely to my destination. When I drive through an intersection, I have faith that other drivers are watching and obeying the signals. When I eat at my favorite restaurant, I have faith that the food was properly prepared and that I will not get sick eating it. I know enough about airplanes, automobiles, and my favorite restaurant to make a rational decision about them.

There are some things, however, that we do not understand, but still act on faith. I do not understand love, but I know it is real. I can't adequately explain electricity, but expect it to help run my computer and keep the lights in my house burning.

In a similar fashion, we don't have to understand all there is to know about Christian faith to embrace it. It takes faith to believe or not believe—but not blind faith. The Silicon Valley business people and scientists whose stories you will read in this section made the effort to examine the abundance of evidence for faith. Ultimately, however, they had to make a decision to believe or not to believe.

Faith is a volitional act. Such an important decision is worth careful consideration. When you think of it, there is no more important decision in life as where to put our faith and trust.

What about doubt? Whether we are looking at the material or spiritual world, we have doubts. I know that planes crash and people don't always obey traffic signals. I have doubts, therefore, that I will get to my destination safely. But if I don't take a step of faith and get on that plane or car, I *know* I will not get to my destination.

Every follower of Christ experiences doubts in his or her faith journey. What is important is what we do about our doubts. We can stay mired in questions and never escape from our doubt, or we can investigate the evidence and decide to take a reasonable step of faith.

The good news is that Christianity lends itself to investigation. In fact, it demands it. There is much historical and archeological evidence, and many books that explore the evidence for Christian faith. Science can shed light on issues of faith as well. The Bible, of course, is the place to begin looking at the evidence. Stories, like those in this section, are also important. We can learn from others' experiences and the evidence they considered in making their decisions for faith.

Chapter 5
Reason and Faith

Faith is taking the first step,
even when you don't see the whole staircase.[1]
~ Dr. Martin Luther King

A common misconception about faith is that it is based only on feelings and emotion, and that reason has little if anything to do with it. Karl Marx famously stated, "Religion is the opiate of the masses."[2] In other words, faith is, in Marx's opinion, a way to anesthetize our minds in order to get through the difficulties of life.

Emotion *is* inextricably tied to Christian faith, and certainly Christian faith provides its adherents a way to navigate the emotional difficulties of life. But Christian faith is much more than that. It is based on evidence and fact.

Faith based only on emotion is like building the foundation of a house on sand. When faith is challenged by the storms of life or by cleverly contrived arguments, faith sinks and is washed away. On the other hand, when faith is based only on fact and intellectual evidence, it never penetrates the essence of what it means to be human. It is head knowledge only, not affecting the behavior and emotions of the individual. Faith based on reason only, results in simply knowing *about* God, not *knowing* God.

With both a strong emotional response to God, including love and gratitude, and a firm intellectual foundation based on the evidence for faith, believers respond with a sense of relief that lifts life's burdens and compels believers to desire not only to know God, but to make God the center of their lives. The result is a desire to surrender one's will to God and a desire to obey His leading.

For these reasons, it makes sense to examine the evidence. We must examine the evidence for faith—that is, use our power of reason—and decide if faith makes sense.

Brent Dusing, an Entrepreneur, Considers the Evidence

Brent Dusing, founder and CEO of Lightside Games, has a big dream for his company. His goal is to reach 100 million people around the world with God's story through entertainment. This is not only a big goal, but a surprising one for a person who over fifteen years ago as an undergraduate at Harvard was, in his words, "not really a believer in Christ." So what changed?

Brent grew up in Missouri. Although he attended church, God was not an important part of his life. He was never part of a youth group and rarely read the Bible. "I always had a clear sense of God," Brent says. "It was always apparent to me that God existed. I just had to look at a sunset or a rainbow, or experience love to know that God or some higher power existed. My issue was that I wanted to do things my way. And I thought that evangelicals were boring and weren't any fun. I didn't want anything to do with them."

At Harvard, Brent grew further away from God. "I attended church only occasionally at first, and then just stopped going. I never read the Bible and was indoctrinated in secular humanism. It was kind of like going into a machine gun fight with a butter knife."

Brent was confronted by many intellectuals on campus claiming that God didn't exist. What surprised Brent was how pervasive secular humanism was at Harvard. "The claim ran across disciplines," comments Brent. "In classes like philosophy, secular humanism was fair game, but the atheist agenda got pushed in literature classes, the biological sciences, psychology, and even in expository writing. It was all anti-Christian. That astounded me."

Brent recalls that as a student in a beginning psychology class, a very bright and articulate professor announced that human behavior was based entirely on nature or nurture, essentially denying the concept of free will. "No one I knew behaved that way," says Brent. "People make their own decisions. It is what our entire political system is based on—free will and self-determination. Here you have this professor saying these things that are just not true. It struck me as false—that biological determinism explains human behavior. And if you tried to challenge him, saying that no one behaves that way, he would say that is just because evolution has worked to convince you that you have free will when you really don't. There was no possibility or shred of credit given in any of my classes to a Christian worldview as having any level of veracity."

Brent's reaction to his experience at Harvard was to set aside his Christian faith during his years at college.

His journey of faith, however, took a sudden turn on a trip to South Africa when he nearly died at the age of 23. The incident happened on a hike where he traversed steep terrain over five different waterfalls. Two hours into the bush, Brent started climbing up chasms between waterfalls. When he reached the fifth waterfall, he slipped and fell twenty feet. "My feet hurt so badly I couldn't stand. I was in excruciating pain." There were no trails and no people in sight. Brent had to make a decision, "Do I sit and wait for help or do I just go back?" Brent couldn't stand without yelling in pain. "But I realized I was in Africa. There were no rescue parties that would come and get me. I had no choice. I pleaded to God for help and started back." He had to climb up and down a cliff face. Since he couldn't stand, he had to sit and paddle down the hill. He finally got out of the bush three to four hours later.

"During that time I was not a Christ-follower by any means," says Brent, "but I felt that God was with me. I don't know any other way to describe it, but He was there with me. I wouldn't have gotten back without Him."

Moves to Silicon Valley—Comes Back to Faith

Two months later Brent came to Silicon Valley to work for Menlo Ventures, a venture capital investment firm. While navigating the complexities of business and life in Silicon Valley, Brent felt that something was missing. "I started feeling guilty for not attending church for so many years." He looked in the Yellow Pages and found the Mountain View Community Church, near where he was living. He began attending services there.

What he heard in the sermons began to make sense to him, but he still wasn't sure about what he believed. So he began a dialog with the church's pastor. "I started asking him questions like: 'Is Jesus really the Son of God?' 'Is the Bible true or just a myth?' 'What about the gods of other religions?'" Brent's pastor was patient, answered what he could, and suggested different books for Brent to read. "Among the most influential books I read were Josh McDowell's *Evidence that Demands a Verdict* and Lee Strobel's *Case for Christ*," Brent says.

Both books fit into a Christian literary category called "apologetics" – meaning a study of the defense or proof of Christian faith. The style of each book is quite different. In *Evidence that Demands a Verdict*, McDowell writes as if he were a defense attorney examining in great detail the evidence for Christian faith. In *Case for Christ*, Strobel takes a journalistic approach, which is his background as a former writer for the *Chicago Tribune*. He interviews several biblical experts, probing them with tough questions to test the validity of the evidence they base their faith on.

In addition to reading McDowell's and Strobel's books, Brent began an in-depth study of the Bible.

Types of Bibles

There are several types of Bibles that are available. One difference among Bibles is the language used in translating the Greek and Hebrew in the original texts. For example, a version translated in the 17th century for the Church of England uses language of that period. It is called the King James Version (KJV). A popular, more modern translation using contemporary English is the New International Version (NIV). And there are several other translations.

Although the biblical text is the same, Bibles are produced for specific audiences. For example, a Mother's Bible provides advice and guidelines for mothers in extra-biblical sidebars and notes. There are Bibles for athletes, business people, teens, children and many other audiences. Another Bible type fits into a category called "Study Bibles," designed to help people study and interpret the meaning of the biblical text. Such Bibles typically provide features, such as maps, cross-references to other parts of the Bible, topical studies on subjects such as prophecy and prayer, and contain commentary by biblical scholars on the history and context of each book of the Bible and key passages.

For his study, Brent chose the *NIV Study Bible* published by Zondervan. The result was profound. "The more I pursued the evidence for God and Christ as the Son of God," says Brent, "the more I found I couldn't deny it. I had been indoctrinated with a secular humanism education in college. I had read Nietzsche, Marx, Weber, Foucault, and many of the famous philosophers. I came to realize that secular humanism is anti-Christian. And at its root, secular humanism is based on opinion and conjecture."

What Brent found particularly compelling were the fulfilled Old Testament prophesies. "Those passages preceded Christ by hundreds of years," says Brent. "Once I held Isaiah 53[3] and Psalm 22[4] up to the Gospel, it became impossible for me to deny God inspired the Bible. So I came to accept the evidence as reliable, and accepted Christ as the Son of God and as my Savior."

The books of Matthew, Mark, Luke, and John—the Gospels—record the details described in Isaiah 53 and Psalm 22, among other prophesies in the Bible. While anyone could argue that one, two, or a handful of prophesies could be mere coincidence, the plethora of Old Testament prophesies—some number in the hundreds—make the likelihood that the prophesies are coincidental infinitely small.

> Scientist Peter Stoner calculated the probability that one man could fulfill only eight of the many Old Testament prophesies about the Messiah. Stoner concludes, "Now these prophecies were either given by inspiration of God or the prophets just wrote them as they thought they should be. In such a case, the prophets had just one chance in 10^{17} of having them come true in any man, but they all came true in Christ."[5]

Brent Becomes an Entrepreneur

After committing to Christian faith and accepting Jesus as his Savior, Brent's life began to change. He started attending church regularly; he made reading the Bible and praying priorities, and he started living out his faith day to day, even at work. At the same time, his career direction began to change.

He left Menlo Ventures to co-found a company he called "Cellfire," and helped build it into one of the nation's leading digital coupon companies. Cellfire is used by leading retail companies, including Walmart, Safeway, and Kroger, having over one billion coupons used to date. Cellfire was sold to Catalina Marketing for $130 million.

Brent left Cellfire after five years to start another company—Lightside Games—to fulfill his desire to build online games. "I always played video games growing up," says Brent, "and thought it would be fun to have a business in games." After experiencing success with the company's first couple of games, Brent realized that there was a big opportunity to make Christian games. The project excited him. "It would merge a lot of what I was passionate about. Our objective was to produce games that were fun, high-quality and biblically authentic." Lightside released its first faith-based game called *Journey of Moses* in August 2011.

Journey of Moses was the first Christian video game on Facebook and was a big hit. The game reached over two million people within two years. The *Journey of Jesus: The Calling* followed. It also attracted over two million players. The company produced *Light the Way: The Bible*, which was produced in conjunction with *The Bible Series*, a smash hit on the History Channel during the 2013 Easter Season. Other games followed, including *Noah's Ark* and *Stained Glass*.

Lightside is well on its way to meet its goal of 100 million users. By the end of 2014, Lightside has had over seven million people play their games. In addition, the evidence points to Lightside attracting people who are not Christians For example, the city with the largest number of players is Cairo, Egypt. And in Turkey, a country with only 70,000 Christians, Lightside has attracted over 100,000 players. Interestingly, a survey conducted by a third party shows that 65% of Muslims who have played Lightside Games have expressed interest in finding out more about Jesus.

When I asked Brent about success, he commented, "What I've learned over time is that God's way is better than my way. It is a process, and I continue to learn that lesson. Success for me is having a positive impact on people's lives." Success for Brent is not just commercial or even influencing people who do not know about faith, but success also means having a positive impact on his family. "When I'm home, and my kids are awake I try my best to invest time with them, do things they enjoy, teach them when possible and just enjoy being with them. I know I will be held accountable to God for how I have used what I have been given. I do my best to use those resources well."

The power of reason was important in Brent Dusing's journey of faith, as it was for most Silicon Valley leaders I have interviewed, including Promod Haque, a top Silicon Valley venture capitalist.

Promod Haque, Venture Capitalist

Promod is a well-known, highly successful venture capitalist. In his 25 years at Norwest Ventures, he has overseen investments in over 60 companies, producing more than $40 billion in value for investors. More than 20 companies have gone public, and many others have been acquired. I met with Promod in his eighth-floor office conference room overlooking downtown Palo Alto and Silicon Valley to discuss his faith journey.

As I gazed out the window waiting for Promod, I realized the significant influence he has had on Silicon Valley technology companies, as well as others around the world.

When he entered the room, I noticed that he is a handsome man in his 60s. He is poised, intelligent, articulate, and friendly.

In 2014, *Forbes Magazine* recognized Promod as a "Hall of Fame" investor. He has appeared on Forbes's annual Midas List of the top venture capitalists 10 times, including in 2004 when he was named Forbes' "number one" venture capitalist. Like others I have interviewed, Promod expressed gratitude for the success he has experienced. "God helped and has blessed me in my career," he says.

Although faith is central to his life today, it was not always. He described himself as "a nominal" Christian when he was growing up in India. "My faith was very ritualistic. We went to church because that's what people did. It was a good experience, but I didn't have a personal relationship with Christ."

That changed at the age of 18 while in engineering school in India. At a meeting run by an organization called "Youth for Christ," a pastor challenged Promod, asking him if he had a personal relationship with Christ. Promod was stunned by the question. It caused him to evaluate his faith. Soon, he says, "I was convicted of my sins and recognized my need to have a savior who would forgive me." The pastor's question prompted Promod to investigate the evidence for faith to validate and strengthen his commitment.

He not only read the Bible, but also read history, including the first-century Jewish historian, Flavius Josephus. Josephus, in his *Antiquities of the Jews* that was published in the first century, mentions Jesus, His crucifixion, the death of John the Baptist, and Jesus' brother, James. Many scholars have used this as one piece of evidence outside of the Bible for Jesus and His crucifixion.

Promod also found the actions of the disciples following resurrection conclusive. "The fact that Jesus's disciples were martyred for what they witnessed and believed was very convincing to me."

Faith is central to Promod's life. Like others in this book, his life changed once he accepted Jesus as his Savior. Today, he views God as is "his CEO" in his business and his life. He remarks:

> *I live by His rules and standards that are absolute. And I take issues like justice, ethics, honesty, and integrity seriously. I work at my job as I am working for Him, not for men. And I fear Him, as that is the beginning of wisdom.*

The Resurrection of Jesus Christ

The resurrection is the foundation of Christian faith. In 1 Corinthians 15, the Apostle Paul describes the centrality of the resurrection to Christian faith: "And if Christ has not been raised, our preaching is useless and so is your faith." Josh McDowell wrote a book called *The Resurrection Factor.*[6] McDowell offers several pieces of evidence that the resurrection is true, including the transformation in the lives of Christ's disciples after Christ's resurrection. The disciples went from cowardly doubters to men who gave their lives for Christ. All died violent deaths for their faith, except John.

Faith and Reason

Faith and reason are not in conflict. People can use their power of reason to weigh the evidence to decide whether or not to take a leap of faith. It is not, however, a gigantic leap if one spends the time and energy to examine the evidence. But even more is at work here. God honors those who sincerely want to find him.

Matthew 7:7-8 reads: "Ask and it will be given to you; seek and you will find; knock and the door will be opened to you. For everyone who asks receives; the one who seeks finds; and to the one who knocks, the door will be opened." The act of seeking—looking at the evidence—is a positive step forward.

What about science? Is there a conflict between faith and science? Let's take a look how some scientists in Silicon Valley deal with the supposed conflict between faith and science.

Chapter 6
Science and Faith

Physical Science does not, in fact, contradict the existence of God.[1]
~ Amir D. Aczel, Mathematician and Scientist

When my daughter, Christina, was in fourth grade she came home one day confused by a comment from one of her classmates: "I believe in science, not God," is what her friend stated. We don't often hear such bold statements directly from people as they get older. Nevertheless, this sentiment is embraced by many. To the skeptic, science and faith are contradictory.

The megaphone on the subject of faith and science seems to belong to the so-called "New Atheists" led by geneticist Dr. Richard Dawkins, along with neuroscientist Dr. Sam Harris, author Christopher Hitchens, and philosopher Dr. Daniel Dennett. "Faith is the great cop-out, the great excuse to evade the need to think and evaluate evidence. Faith is belief in spite of, even perhaps because of, the lack of evidence,"[2] says Dawkins.

Others disagree.

Award-winning mathematician and scientist Amir D. Aczel, profoundly disagrees with the New Atheists' view of science and faith. In fact, he believes their views pose a danger to science. In his 2014 book *Why Science Does Not*

Disprove God, he takes the arguments of the New Atheists head on. He writes, "The purpose of this book is to defend the integrity of science."[3] Although it is not clear from the book what faith tradition, if any, Aczel follows, he makes it clear that both science and faith have important roles to play in our lives. "Science and spirituality are both integral parts of the human search for truth and meaning; they provide us possible paths of comprehending and appreciating the vast cosmos and our place in it." Aczel covers topics including the origins of the universe, evolution, archeology, mathematics, probability and God, and quantum physics in making his case.

Nobel Prize nominee and physical scientist Dr. Henry F. Schaefer, in his book *Science and Christianity: Conflict or Coherence?*[4] specifically addresses Christian faith and science. Schaefer begins by citing a study that shows that the number of scientists who are believers is proportionally the same as the population at large. He then offers a historical perspective on science and Christianity by listing a host of renowned scientists who were believers in Jesus Christ. These early scientists pursued their craft as a way to discover and understand God's creation. Schaefer quotes Newton, Pascal, Boyle, Bacon, Faraday, Maxwell, and many other scientific pioneers as believing Christians.

Schaefer goes on to list modern scientists who are believers as well. For example, he quotes Allan Sandage, who is considered the world's greatest living cosmologist: "The world is too complicated in all its parts and interconnections to be due to chance alone. I am convinced that the existence of life with all its order is simply too well put together."

Schaefer describes how modern scientific thinking confirms the biblical explanations for life and the world around us. For example, Schaefer explains how the Big Bang theory offers the most plausible and most widely accepted scientific explanation for the beginning of the universe and how that theory dovetails with the creation story in Genesis. Schaefer also refutes on scientific grounds the theories of renowned, non-believing scientists like Carl Sagan and Stephen Hawking.

What about scientists in Silicon Valley?

Dr. David Persing

One is Dr. David Persing. Like scientists before him, Dr. Persing's passion is to apply his God-given talents, training in science, and his experience to make a positive impact on the world. His specialty is molecular diagnostics. As the executive vice president and chief medical and technology officer at Cepheid, a rapidly growing molecular diagnostics company, he is living out his passion to "do well by doing good."

David was born and raised in Silicon Valley. He graduated Magna Cum Laude with a Chemistry degree from San Jose State University and was accepted into a prestigious 8-year training program leading to MD and PhD degrees in genetics from the University of California, San Francisco. He did his medical residency at the Yale University School of

Medicine before being drawn to do clinical practice and research work in infectious diseases at the Mayo Clinic in Rochester, Minnesota.

As the founder and director of the Molecular Microbiology laboratory at the Mayo Clinic, David had the opportunity to establish one of the first labs in the country dedicated to the development of a revolutionary technique used in medical and biological research called "Polymerase Chain Reaction," or PCR. After working for nine years at the Mayo Clinic, he left academic research in 1999 to join Corixa, a Seattle-based biotech company, to pursue translational research in cancer and infectious diseases. In 2005, David was recruited to join Cepheid in Sunnyvale, California, where he leads the company's development efforts in the use of PCR as a breakthrough technology for detecting infectious diseases and cancer.

Along the way, David co-authored the first textbook on molecular testing, *Molecular Microbiology: Diagnostic Principles and Practice*. The book is in its third edition and has become the standard teaching textbook in the field. In addition, David has written hundreds of scholarly articles, some of which have appeared in high-impact journals such as *Science* and the *New England Journal of Medicine*.

Faith Background

David grew up as a follower of Christ. As a youngster, he attended the Saratoga Federated Church in Saratoga, California. In high school, a youth pastor took David and a small group of high school students under his wing and brought them to L'Abri (French for "the Shelter"), where students studied issues of faith with Christian luminaries such as Francis Schaeffer (founder of L'Abri) and Os Guinness. David remarks, "We would sit for hours at the feet of Francis Schaeffer, transfixed by discussions of faith, science and reason. It was an incredible experience to discuss issues of faith in depth and to realize that to be a Christian one did not have to commit intellectual suicide."

As a sophomore in college, David went on a short-term mission trip to Guatemala sponsored by his church. It was a life-changing experience for David. He met a local doctor who asked David for help delivering a baby that night. "I had gloves on," says David, "but they were work gloves. They were crusted in cement from the reconstruction work I was doing. The doctor told me he had rubber gloves more suitable for the task and just needed an extra pair of hands for the delivery. The delivery went fine. I ended up working every night with the doctor during the mission trip. At that point, I was hooked and decided to do pre-med in college."

> It was an incredible experience to discuss issues of faith in depth and to realize that to be a Christian one did not have to commit intellectual suicide.

While in college, David worked part time at San Jose Hospital in the clinical lab and the X-ray room, which David says, "was my first exposure to the power of diagnostics." He and other students also raised money and obtained donated equipment to set up a lab and X-ray facility in Guatemala where he traveled periodically during the rest of his college years.

Faith Challenged—Creation versus Evolution

In graduate school, David's faith was challenged. "Up to that point I had not thought much about origins and the evolution versus creation argument," says David. "In graduate school it became clear to me that the relatedness of species was borne out not just by phenotype descriptions, but also at the genetic level. There were convincing arguments about the evolutionary process which challenged my earlier assumptions—what I believed about creation and what I was seeing in DNA sequencing showing the evolution of species."

Having a front-row seat in the study of DNA and genetics and having a solid background in Christian theology forced David to undertake further critical thinking in this area.

> *Ultimately I spent a lot of time reading in an attempt to reconcile creation and evolution. I came to the conclusion that science and faith are not at all incompatible. Someone once said that all truth is God's truth, and I believe that. I came away with a greater understanding of the complexity of creation—the idea that God could build plasticity into the genome with the ability to adapt and change and be molded into new forms and new*

> *species. I realized that the genome is not a fixed entity. There is good evidence that it is fluid and can change in the context of new environmental conditions and that the basic principles of Darwinian Natural Selection are true. I just preferred to think of it as "Supernatural Selection."*

Where David parts ways with traditional evolutionary theorists is that he believes that the evolutionary process is not random. If evolution was random, as secular scholars believe, no God is required. "I view the plasticity of the genome as a critical design element coming from an intelligent entity to create new features and properties. The combination of that inherent flexibility, with the concept of a supernaturally guided form of Darwinian evolution, is how I see the fit between creation and evolution."

At the same time, David takes issue with Christians in the Intelligent Design camp. In doing so, David agrees with the thinking of fellow Christian Francis Collins. Collins is a former atheist and physician-geneticist who headed the Human Genome Project for the National Institute for Health (NIH) for 12 years before accepting an appointment by President Obama as the director of NIH in 2009. Collins wrote a popular book, *The Language of God: A Scientist Presents Evidence for Belief,* [5] in which he provides both his journey of faith and his explanation of how God used evolution. Collins views science and faith this way: "Science's domain is to explore nature. God's domain is in the spiritual world, a realm not possible to explore with the tools and language of science. It must be examined with the heart, mind, and the soul—and the mind must find a way to embrace both realms."[6]

David Persing and Francis Collins adhere to a philosophy some call "theistic evolution," although Collins prefers to use the term "BiosLogos." It is important to understand that believing Christians differ on their view of creation and evolution. Some view Genesis 1 and 2 literally, believing creation occurred in seven 24-hour days, while others view the term "day" to mean a period of time, as it sometimes does in English usage. Others view Genesis 1 and 2 as allegorical.

It should be recognized, however, that although believing Christians can differ in their view of creation, they hold firm to their belief in God as the Creator. God exists outside of time and space and is responsible for creating the universe and man. Personally, I look forward to learning the answers to these and other questions when I am with God.

Faith and Work

When Persing joined Cepheid, he was around 50 years old. He felt that he had 15 to 20 years left in his career to make a major impact. "I wanted to express my faith through my work," says Persing. He wanted to have not only a local impact on individual patients, but a worldwide impact. He saw that opportunity at Cepheid. "One of the ideas we had discussed early on was to address one of the world's most deadly diseases, tuberculosis (TB), and bring much-needed molecular testing to the masses." He saw the potential to take the PCR methods he worked on at the Mayo Clinic, and apply them to medical needs. "I saw the opportunity to take what looked like a silicon wafer fabrication facility at Mayo—highly trained personnel running around in gowns, masks, hoods, and gloves in four laboratories—and make it all happen in a small, automated cartridge. The impact would be to bring this sophisticated technology to a much broader audience—essentially to democratize the technology."

The first opportunity came with a grant from the Foundation for Innovative Diagnostics (FIND) in Geneva with funding from the Bill and Melinda Gates Foundation to develop, with collaborators at New Jersey Medical School, a revolutionary approach to detecting tuberculosis (TB). TB treatment presented a challenge to conventional methods, as the techniques were either insensitive or took months to get a diagnosis. With the technology from Cepheid called the "Xpert MTB/Rif Test," the diagnosis could be done inexpensively and in two hours by nearly anyone, in any setting.

Although the spread of TB is under control in the U.S., it is a major problem in the rest of the world, especially in developing areas like Africa, India, and Asia. TB kills approximately 150 million people annually. Getting a quick, inexpensive diagnosis would not only help the people with TB to get them on the correct treatment sooner, but could also curtail the spread of the disease.

Cepheid's Xpert MTB/Rif test for TB was introduced in 2010. By early 2015, approximately 10 million tests had been run, and the number continues to grow. The volume has now reached a level where there is no longer a need for subsidies from international aid agencies. The tests cost less than $10.00 to administer.

TB testing is not the only product using the PCR process at Cepheid. The outbreak of Ebola in West Africa dominated medical news in 2014. Under the direction of David, Cepheid looked at ways to apply its PCR technology to early detection of the disease. "The problem with Ebola," says David, "is that people with fevers are often put in the same room for days until the medical staff determine who is infected with Ebola and who is not." In this situation, the Ebola can easily spread to people uninfected with the virus. Early detection is necessary.

In March, 2015, Cepheid's PCR detection for Ebola was approved for emergency use in regions affected by Ebola. With Cepheid's low-cost Ebola test, workers can detect Ebola in less than two hours, "often as little as one hour," explains David. Lives will be saved, and Ebola has a chance to be controlled.

Cepheid is also working to detect other diseases, including cancer and sexually transmitted diseases like HIV.

Fulfilling His Life's Dream

For Persing, working at Cepheid and impacting the world for good is a dream come true. "It is fulfilling to see my faith expressed through my work, and how that is playing out. It has been an absolute dream to see this happen. I am gratified to be one of the forces of democratization of this technology across the world. It fits with Catholic social teaching about care for the poor and is a genuine expression of my faith. In a sense, my work is my prayer."

Dr. Phil Stillman

"Doing well by doing good" is a common theme among scientists and others I interviewed who are followers of Christ. They want to apply their talents to helping others. Dr. Phil Stillman is an anesthesiologist at El Camino Hospital in Mountain View, California. He views his work in medicine as his ministry. Phil not only works hard at his profession, but he also takes the time to get to know his patients and prays for them. In addition, he uses his off hours and vacation time for medical missions and other volunteer work.

Phil was not always a follower of Christ. He grew up in a non-religious home in Saratoga, California, an expensive town at the foot of the Santa Cruz Mountains. But as a teenager, he began to think about faith, prompted by his concern about the Vietnam War and turbulent times in the 1970s. "I didn't know my purpose in life," he says. "I was thinking about the war, possibly dying and what would happen after I died."

Phil began to research faith and religion on his own, reading several books including the Bible and *Mere Christianity* by C.S. Lewis. He also attended a Bible study and found a friend who was willing to answer his questions about Christian faith. But he needed more evidence to see if Christianity was true. After reading several books, including *Evidence that Demands a Verdict* by Josh McDowell, Phil felt confident in the evidence for Christianity. He says, "The Bible stories have all been supported both by archeology and history. And the scriptures have survived over 3,000 years intact confirmed by the Isaiah scrolls at Qumran and many other documents."

After much research and contemplation, Phil accepted Christ into his life at a Billy Graham crusade when he was 18 years old. Today, he practices his faith consistently. Each day he takes time to pray for his patients and personally minister to those he can. He has adopted John 10:10 in the Bible as a verse he lives by. In that verse, Jesus says, "I have come that they may have life and have it in full." Phil remarks, "My life has certainly been abundant. It's been a lot of risk taking, a lot of failures but with tremendous abundance and joy. I'm very much like C. S. Lewis in that sometimes I'm just surprised by joy. I'm so glad that I chose to follow Jesus Christ."

Living out one's faith is not always easy. Phil intimates that he is sometimes challenged by his medical colleagues for what he believes. However, he hasn't wavered. "They just don't get it," he says. "To me, a life in Christ is pure joy.

I'm just so happy to be a Christian. People sometimes say that I'm crazy, but so be it. That's just the way it is."

Applies His Skills in Medical Missions Work

Phil often uses his vacation time to volunteer for medical missions work overseas. His first missions trip was to Guatemala during the summer after his first year of medical school. "It was a great time. Every day was a new experience. I got the bug for missions work on that trip." A few years later, Phil was asked to go on another trip to Guatemala. He says, "I just get this call out of the blue from this guy I don't know in Bakersfield. He said, 'We're going to Guatemala, do you want to come?' I replied, 'Yes.' He was surprised. It turns out they were desperate for an anesthesiologist, and he was just cold calling people, and I was the second person he called. It was like God just engineered the whole thing." Phil went on the trip and enjoyed a wonderful time, and since then has taken several more medical missions trips to Guatemala and Ethiopia.

Most believing scientists, like David and Phil, are secure in their faith. They simply go about their work fulfilling what they sense is God's mission for them. Others, like Amir Aczel, Francis Schaeffer, and Francis Collins felt the need to fight back against the conventional wisdom that says that science and faith are not compatible. They wrote books and accept invitations to speak.

Paul Baba, Scientist, Businessman, and Follower of Christ

Dr. Paul Baba is a now-retired Silicon Valley scientist and businessman who also felt the need to speak out. He wrote a book called *All the Evidence You Will Ever Need: A Scientist Believes in the Gospel of Jesus Christ*. In his book, Paul lays out the evidence for Christ and Christian faith.

In 1960, Paul earned his PhD in Ceramics Science from the Rutgers University College of Engineering. Upon graduation, he worked as a research scientist at Bell Labs in New Jersey, one of the top research organizations in the world at the time. There he specialized in magnetic ceramics for computer memory applications. Paul came to Silicon Valley in 1965 when Ampex Corporation recruited him to manage the development of innovative magnetic materials for tape recorder heads and microwave materials. Later he worked in senior management roles at Integrated Automation and Litton Industries, among other companies. At Integrated Automation, his division pioneered the field of document imaging.

Faith Background

Paul declares that he has been a follower of Christ for over 65 years. It was at a youth camp that he answered an invitation to accept Christ as his Savior. In his book, Paul describes his experience this way. "It was not emotional; there were no thunderclaps or bolts of lightning. It was a simple logical decision. My life was changed forever—not perfection—at times I still did things I was ashamed of, but there was a clear change of direction."[7]

His faith was challenged along the way. He recalls a particular trial he encountered in college. "A professor in a geology class devoted his last lecture to items intended to undermine faith. And he allowed no questions, opinions, or discussion. As time went by, I looked at the evidence and learned to answer the opinions presented by the professor. Gradually my understanding and faith grew."

Compelled to Present the Evidence

After Paul had retired from business, he felt compelled to lay out the abundant evidence for Christian faith. He is careful to point out that evidence alone does not "prove" the existence of God or the divinity of Jesus. But as in a legal trial or well-designed scientific investigation, the evidence is convincing. Paul even suggests a process—a set of questions—that a skeptic should consider as he or she investigates the evidence for faith.

- Is there an intelligent designer? If there is,
- Did the Creator leave us with a manual? If the Bible is the manual,
- What does the Bible tell us about the way to eternal life?

Paul concludes, "Our faith is not blind faith. Taken together all the evidence is convincing. But each of us has to decide for ourselves. No one can prove beyond a doubt that God exists or that Jesus is the Son of God. If these things could be proven beyond doubt, we would not need faith. The evidence is there if one takes the time to investigate."

What about Miracles?

The Apostle Paul calls the resurrection the pivotal point of Christian faith.[8] If Christ did not rise from the dead, Christian faith is meaningless.

The resurrection, of course, violates the natural order. People do not resurrect after they die. The resurrection is a miracle—the central miracle of Christian faith. There are, of course, many other miracles in the Bible, including the virgin birth, the parting of the Red Sea, and the unexplainable healing of the blind and lepers by Jesus.

What are we to make of miracles? What do scientists steeped in the study of natural phenomena think about miracles—true miracles, not what people sometimes call miracles—like the birth of a child, a beautiful sunrise, an unexpected windfall. Those things can be explained. But what about events we cannot explain by science? Paul Baba looks at miracles this way:

> *There are different categories of miracles. Sometimes miracles can be explained by natural causes but are considered miracles because of the*

timing of the event. Consider the parting of the sea for Moses and the Israelites. Certainly, wind could have caused such an event, but why did it happen when Moses and the Israelites needed to cross and then stopped when the Egyptians tried to cross? Natural causes can not explain other miracles. But if there is an all-powerful God, why couldn't He perform miracles?

The primary objection to the possibility of miracles comes from the belief that science can not explain miracles. It is correct to say that science cannot explain miracles, but it does not follow that miracles, therefore, are impossible. Science deals with the natural world in which events are repeated and tested. Miracles, however, are not natural; they are supernatural.

In Section 3: Struggle, Adversity, and Faith, you will read stories about some people who experienced miracles. But first we will look at the story of Stanford consulting professor, Dr. William Hurlbut, and learn how he sees the intersection of faith and science.

Chapter 7
The Search for Truth

We know the truth, not only by reason, but by the heart.[1]
~ Blaise Pascal

The search for truth is common in the stories of people chronicled in this book and in the lives of most people. "Who is God?" "Can I know God?" "Is the Bible true?" These are the questions people struggle with on their spiritual journeys.

The pursuit of truth is the preoccupation of all deep thinkers. Theologians of all faiths look for truth in the ancient documents they peruse and the interactions of life they observe. Philosophers search for truth in their quest for explanations for reality and existence. Scientists look for truth in the natural and physical world through experimentation and observation.

Dr. William Hurlbut is a physician and consulting professor at Stanford University. He has spent much of his life searching for truth—both scientific and theological truth, and the intersection of the two.

In preparation of my meeting with Dr. Hurlbut, I studied his background and reviewed several scholarly articles he published. It was clear to me that he was a deep thinker about both science and faith, and particularly about the direction of science and its ethical implications.

Having arrived early for my meeting with Dr. Hurlbut, I strolled through the Stanford campus before settling on a bench, sipping a cup of coffee. It was a beautiful spring morning with the sounds of chirping birds filling the air. As I watched students hurrying off to class—some on foot, others streaming quickly by on their bicycles—my thoughts turned to the privilege students and professors enjoy at Stanford and other campuses, and the opportunity they have to step away from daily life to explore intellectual issues, including the search for truth. I wondered in particular how an intellectual stalwart like Dr. William Hurlbut came to a deep faith in Christ, how science informed his search for spiritual truth, and the role faith played in his quest for scientific truth.

I wasn't sure what to expect when I met Dr. Hurlbut, but I was pleasantly surprised to find him disarmingly affable. As we settled into his cramped office with walls lined with books, he asked that I call him "Bill." From his warmth I could tell he enjoyed people and the opportunity to engage in conversation.

In the interview I discovered that Bill was one of the most popular professors at Stanford. His undergraduate classes on bioethics that he had taught for many years were continuously oversubscribed, as is his current course on the same subject that he teaches for the Department of Neurobiology at Stanford Medical School.

By its nature the subject of bioethics, which deals with beginning and end of life issues and subjects like cloning, is controversial. At one point in the interview, Bill displayed for me a thick notebook full of supportive letters he received from students when some on the faculty who disagreed with his bioethical position on certain issues sought to have him removed from the university. He survived the ordeal with the backing of the Stanford President who told Bill that he was moved by the overwhelming support he received from the students.

Bill's Background

Bill grew up in a suburb of New York City in a family with a Stanford tradition. His entire nuclear family attended Stanford, as did 18 of his relatives. His dad worked as a medical doctor. Coming from a family that valued education and what he calls "productive engagement in the world," Bill's curiosity was naturally raised on several subjects. "At Stanford," he says, "I wanted to understand the world, so I took courses in many areas."

Although he says that his parents were not particularly religious, they valued faith and wanted to expose their children to the study of the divine. "I was sort of shoved out the door and told to go to Sunday School," Bill says. He attended Sunday School and worship services regularly as he grew up.

At Stanford, however, he attended religious services only sporadically during his first three years, and never cracked the Bible he was given. An event his senior year changed all that.

Although not a political radical, he was interested in exploring the counter-cultural world he saw emerging in the 1960s. One day in his senior year, he watched an angry crowd protesting leaders of Hewlett-Packard and Bank of America for "crimes against the world" and as "enemies of the people." His initial reaction was to laugh at the protestors he called "opportunists who didn't have the virtue of starting productive companies."

His second reaction, however, was to go home to the little cottage he was renting, and pull out his Bible. "I am not sure why I did that," he says, "but I knew that the problems were deeper than just social change. It was clear to me that you had to change the heart of a person to get at deep problems, and the answers had to be very deep for there to be any real transformation." The Bible, he reasoned, could give him some answers.

Bill started his Bible reading with the Gospel of Matthew, and he continued with his study over the next several months. He was so intellectually stirred by what he read that he got down on his knees one day and told God, "I don't understand any of this for sure. I don't even know if it is real. Please make it plain." The next six months he says "were like a storm."

> *Everything that I knew, including all my understanding of history – the history of ideas, the history of political events, all started to take shape. I started to understand medieval philosophy that I had studied but hadn't understood. I started to*

> *understand why there were religious wars, and, although it wasn't right, what they were fighting over; why the missionaries had gone where they went, and why science had developed the way it did. It all started to make sense to me.*

Once convinced of the fundamental reality of faith, Bill looked for a Christian community to help him better understand his nascent Christian faith. The church at Stanford did not meet his needs, so he went outside the campus. He found the Peninsula Bible Church (PBC) in Palo Alto, where he says, he was "nourished." At PBC, he consistently attended Sunday worship services and credits the pastors of the church—Ray Stedman, Ron Ritchie, and Dave Roper—with helping him get a hold of his newly found beliefs.

But ever the curious student, he wanted to understand the historical roots of Christianity and the reasons for denominational variations. "We have gotten into a lot of problems in the modern world with fundamentalism." He notes that people read the Bible with different interpretations. Some of the Bible is historical and is to be taken literally; in other cases the language is poetical and metaphorical. "Even more than metaphorical," he says, "the Bible is about mysterious things that are hard to put in everyday language. The challenge is to read the Bible consistently."

At the same time as he was exploring biblical truth, he also found career direction. In his undergraduate studies he gravitated toward biology and medicine. "I thought that is where the real drama is—where you get to think about what life is and why we are here." Since he didn't have enough pre-med course by the time he graduated, he took a fifth year and then entered the Medical School.

At medical school, Bill developed a growing concern about the coming biological revolution that he says was marked by the invention and commercialization of the birth control pill. "Regardless of what is right or wrong, practical or impractical, one has to admit that the birth control pill was like an earthquake in our social morality. It struck me as one trained in medicine that for the first time in human history we were prescribing to tens of millions of people a drug that was not intended to cure a disease but to counteract a natural capacity of the body. That was a thoroughly significant departure from the kind of medicine that prevailed at the time."

In his last year at medical school, his wife gave birth to his first child who suffered brain damage during delivery due to mistakes by the medical team. Because of that tragedy along with the revival of his spiritual quest and his predilection for thinking about the big issues of life, Bill decided not to take the typical route of a medical school graduate. Instead of entering a residency program, he decided to engage in a post-doctoral study in theology and medical ethics at Stanford.

"I wanted to know the truth," he says. "Why are we here? And what is life on earth about? It is kind of divine pedagogy. We learn who we are, and why we experience struggles and joy." He was also troubled by the implications of genetic engineering he saw coming. Most importantly, he wanted to understand Christian history. "I wanted to understand why St. Francis gave up his wealth, why the early monks went off to the desert alone, why Martin de Porres, the Peruvian saint, whipped his own back, and so on. And I wanted to understand how to make sense of the Bible in the real world."

Truth

Truth means conformity with reality. Reality is something we can test and experience. In the case of God, truth means trustworthy. The Bible talks much about truth. Jesus says, "In fact, the reason I was born and came into the world is to testify to the truth. Everyone on the side of truth listens to me."[2] And knowing the truth is a freeing experience. Jesus says, "If you hold to my teaching, you really are my disciples. Then you will know the truth, and the truth will set you free."[3]

Bill's study of theology and medical ethics extended beyond his course work at Stanford; he also studied with Louis Bouyer of the Institute Catholique de Paris. In addition, he studied Human Vitae, Pope Paul VI's encyclical on human life and birth control.

Upon completion of his course work, he was awarded a Post-doctoral Fellowship to study with the Dean of Stanford Memorial Church, Robert Hamerton-Kelly. That was the beginning of a "forty-year conversation" that lasted until the Dean's death in 2013. That dialogue was a crucial continuation of his quest for truth, especially in the intersection of faith and science. Today, Bill not only teaches at Stanford, but writes scholarly, thought-provoking articles and is a sought-after speaker.

On Evolution and Faith

The compatibility of evolution and faith is a common stumbling block for seekers of faith. The central issue is the reconciliation of faith with the linchpin of evolution—"the survival of the fittest." Morality, self-sacrifice, and love do not fit into this core element. Bill addresses the apparent incompatibility in a scholarly 2001 article in the *Journal of Psychology and Theology* titled "Evolutionary Theory and the Emergence of Moral Nature." In the article, Bill writes: "Evolution is a useful theoretical tool for understanding many dimensions of biology, but is not the ultimate arbiter of issues of metaphysics, and is not religion (though some of its advocates haul all of reality up to this altar)."[4]

Evolutionary psychology, he says, provides some insights, "… but its initial narrow set of assumptions derive not from scientific evidence but represent philosophical and theological views."[5] Evolutionary psychology has nothing to say about design, purpose, and meaning. "The practical effect of this is to reduce all human behaviors to value-neutral adaptations (i.e., having no general reference to transcendent truths) and deny the spiritual significance of mind and moral culture."[6] "…This incompatibility, however, stems not from irreconcilable differences, but from an over-extension and misapplication of the methodology of evolutionary psychology…"[7]

According to evolutionary psychology, concepts like cooperation, morality, altruism, and self-sacrifice are derived from inherited traits to keep genetic material intact, resulting in sustainability of the human species. But Bill finds the arguments unsatisfying. Instead, he reframes the understanding of the evolution of morality "…such that the central claims of both perspectives are at once preserved and lifted to a higher and more integrated level of description."[8]

In the article, Bill goes on to explore how the concepts like flexibility and freedom in thought, empathy, and love—so central to human nature—are only adequately explained by the existence of the loving God who exhorts us to "Seek first his kingdom and his righteousness."[9]

He comments:

> *The entire cosmic order of time and space and material being may be seen as an arena for the revelation of Love, for the creation of a creature capable of ascending to an appreciation of its Creator; but more profoundly, for the reaching down, the compassionate condescension of Love, Himself.*[10]

Bill concludes by offering what he sees as the compatibility of evolutionary theory and Christian faith.

> *Christianity may at once affirm the reality of positive significance in the evolutionary process. In the emergence of moral nature, humanity is called into communion with the very life of God, the life of Love.*[11]

On Suffering and Redemption

"How could a loving God allow suffering?" This question is a barrier to many as they consider faith. Bill uses Giovanni Francesco di Bernardone or St. Francis of Assisi as he is commonly known, the 13th century monk, to help answer this question. Francis understood God's desire to be in union with us. By living a life in poverty, in oneness with nature, and by experiencing physical pain, he drew closer to Christ. Bill comments, "Indeed, Francis had prayed that he would know the pain of the passion of his Lord, in order to comprehend more fully the depth and meaning of God's love."[12]

Although Francis's desire to suffer may seem extreme to us in the modern world, there is a deep meaning for Christians that comes with suffering. Christ became man to suffer and die so that anyone who puts their trust in Him will be saved. Christ's torture and death on the cross are acts of ultimate love for humanity. Bill writes, "Through the eyes of faith, the entire cosmic order of time and space and material being may be seen as an arena for the revelation of Love… The fullness of Love was revealed in human form. In that moment of human history, the entirety of creation was lifted to another level of meaning. The evolutionary struggle, the seeming futility of suffering and sacrifice and death itself, was raised to the possibility of participation in a higher order of being."[13]

In St. Francis, Bill sees someone we can learn from today. "He [Francis] came to see that the whole creation, and each of its varied creatures in their distinct strengths and struggles, reflected and revealed the perfection of the Creator."[14] And in Francis's frame of mind, Bill sees limits on the modern use of biotechnology. "Recognition of the fragile interdependence of living nature urges us to be cautious—lest we disrupt the basic balance of being and thereby drain the created order of its beauty, vitality, and spiritual significance."[15]

On Bioethics and the Role of Medicine

"Biotechnology," Bill says, "is more than a set of ingenious processes and products. It is also a conceptual and ethical outlook grounded in ideas about the source and significance of the natural world, an outlook informed by philosophical assumptions about progress and human destiny."[16] Although Bill has dedicated much of his life to the study of bioethical issues, he does not call himself a "bioethicist." He says that bioethics is not a profession, but a conversation that requires the perspectives of the whole community. For his part, he considers himself to be a physician and citizen who is trying to understand the implications of medical and scientific technological advancements, and simply wants to have a voice in the wider conversation about biotechnology and ethics.

In March 2015, Bill presented Grand Rounds at the Mayo Clinic in Rochester, Minnesota, on the topic "Professional or Provider: Biotechnology, Suffering, and Human Aspiration." Grand Rounds meetings are conducted to help medical professionals increase their knowledge. In his talk, he addressed the changing role of medicine due to technological breakthroughs, the way medicine has gone from curing disease, alleviating suffering, and restoring the patient to normal functioning and wellbeing, to helping patients in their quest for happiness and human perfection. The physician's role becomes "a new agenda, the technological extension of human desires and dreams."[17]

The prescription of diet pills, Viagra ®, growth hormones, and procedures like liposuction and breast implants are well-known examples. Human cloning and research in the conquest of aging are more controversial examples. His concerns, which are informed by his Christian faith, extend to his respect for human dignity and what will become of civilization. He cites two examples he noticed in the news just prior to his talk that bookend human life—issues related to birth and death.

The first was a new "three parent embryo" procedure in which the maternal embryo created by the parents is altered by adding material from a donor embryo that is sacrificed in the process. His concern is for the destroyed embryo—which he and many call human life—and for the implications for wide-spread human engineering.

Bill's second example was for a heavily funded research project using human embryos for cloning to help extend human life and for projects to attempt to end death. The research is being conducted by a colleague of Bill's in laboratory sites in China, a country that does not have stringent bioethical laws. Bill comments, "If we create and destroy human embryos for the purposes of a technological project—no matter how noble our intentions—we fracture the very foundation on which all other moral principles and practices are built."[18]

He concludes by saying, "As we enter now into this new age of biomedical technology, we must resist the pressures to become mere providers at the service of the will of others. Rather, we must sustain the central meaning of medicine through our calling as true professionals; the very survival of our civilization may depend on us."[19]

Although his conclusion may sound alarmist, Bill cites the possibility that nation-states could harness biotechnology and neuro-technology in coercive programs of social engineering and social control in the name of creating a better world.[20] Perhaps equally disturbing, he notes, is that free-enterprising people with well-intended desires to improve human life could "break the very connections and conditions that are the solid foundation of flourishing and sources of our deepest sense of significance and satisfaction."[21]

Bill Hurlbut's desire for truth, together with his faith and calling as a scientist and physician, led him to the investigation and ethical considerations for the use of biotechnology. As he continues on his path for truth, he recognizes that the full understanding for truth is limited in this life. He acknowledges the many instances when scientists thought they knew truth, only to have their thinking overturned by new discoveries.

"Science and faith are not opposed to each other," relates Bill. "Many of the great discoveries of science were made by Christians." He cites Roger Bacon who was a Franciscan, and Thomas Aquinas and Albert Magnus who were Dominicans. "There is no coincidence that the early foundations of science have their roots in Christian faith… Science is really a little parenthetical clause within a larger description of reality. Science is like an island in a larger sea of truth. You can't completely explain the world by science; you need spiritual understanding as well. And it is not right to think that there is a distinction between spiritual and material truth—they were poured forth from the same creative source. They are ultimately one and the same."

Neither followers of Christ nor agnostics should fear the search for truth. God made us with minds to think and with a curious nature to explore both the world around us and the meaning of our existence.

Science is a discipline, ordained by God, to understand the workings of His creation. Science, for example, can help explain the creative process, as it strives to do with the Big Bang theory and evolution. The application of scientific principles also helps God's children live longer with more productive and better lives.

Science, however, can also be manipulated for destructive purposes—nuclear and chemical weapons and genetic engineering are examples. Faith provides a framework in which to discuss the ethical implications of the application of science. Dr. Bill Hurlbut is not only a voice in that discussion, but serves as an example of a person endowed with an inquisitive mind who gives credence to the intersection between scientific and theological truth.

Section Three: Struggle, Pain, and Faith

God whispers to us in our pleasures, speaks in our conscience, but shouts in our pain: it is His megaphone to rouse a deaf world.[1]
~ C.S. Lewis

Everyone faces struggle, adversity, and pain in their lives. People of faith are not immune. In fact, the Apostle Peter tells us that we should expect it.[2] The subject of pain raises many questions. Why does a loving God allow pain? Why does He allow a child to die? Why does he allow people to suffer from cancer? These are good questions with no simple answers.

Theologians would argue that pain and struggle came into this world when Adam and Eve rebelled against God. They would also say that God is not the creator of pain and suffering. However, God does allow pain. While theologically true from a Christian perspective, such arguments do not particularly help the person suffering. The distinction between creating and allowing pain is irrelevant. Pain is real, and it hurts.

Pain impacts our lives in powerful and unexpected ways. For a surgeon to heal a person with a ruptured appendix, he must cut the person to remove the unhealthy organ. In the same way, God sometimes allows pain to get our attention so that we can correct an unhealthy behavior. Pain often drives people to pray and to search the Bible for answers. In the process, people can deepen their relationship with Him. The Bible tells us that pain and struggle also build perseverance, character, and hope,[3] and that good comes out of struggle for those who believe.[4]

Some people allow struggle and pain to drive them away from God. Pain often results in anger and can grow into bitterness. Some reject God outright as a result of pain.

As with many spiritual issues, the question of pain forces us to decide. Do we reject God as unloving due to our pain, or do we trust in His promises? In the Bible, God promises that He will take care of our every need, that He is with us in our pain, and that all things work together for good for those who trust in Him. Do we rely on those promises, or do we dismiss them?

In the first section of the book, we explored the interaction between success and faith in the stories of certain Silicon Valley leaders. In the second section, we saw how Christian faith lends itself to investigation, is central to the search for truth, and serves as a motivation for believers to use their personal gifts and talents to make a difference in the world. In this section, we explore the significant role struggle and pain play in finding faith, deepening one's relationship with God, and in discovering meaning and purpose.

In this section, you will read the journeys of Silicon Valley leaders who faced struggle and pain. Some overcame their adversity through prayer and even experienced miracles. The prayers of others did not seem to get answered, at least not as they wanted. They continued to endure pain. Some even lost loved ones. In their pain, they wrestled with God for answers. But in their struggle, each person found something valuable—a deeper relationship with the Creator of the Universe.

Chapter 8
Peace in the Face of Adversity

It's not whether you get knocked down. It's whether you get up.[1]
~ Vince Lombardi, Coach, Green Bay Packers

The offices of National Exchange Services (NES) in downtown San Jose provide a picturesque view of the city. The offices overlook a palm tree-lined courtyard between San Jose's finest hotel, The Fairmont, and the Museum of Modern Art. This serene and peaceful setting is a fitting metaphor for the attitude NES's founder and president, Michael Halloran, displayed when he faced a perfect storm of adversity beginning in 2001.

A failed merger put the company he was leading at the time, H Marketing Services, on the verge of bankruptcy. His personal assets were exhausted. And he had a growth on his brain that doctors told him would lead to almost certain death if not removed, or if removed, would likely lead to paralysis.

Michael's strong Christian faith helped him face this pending catastrophe with hope and confidence that no matter what the result—even death or financial ruin—God would use it for good. How can someone faced with such adversity stay strong? From where does such faith come?

Michael says, “There was never a day in my life that I remember not believing in God.” At an early age he understood that Jesus came to forgive us and to die for our sins. He grew up in Southern California and attended a Lutheran church regularly with his parents. “Faith,” he says, “was part of my DNA.” Even throughout college, a time in life when many question their faith, Michael never did.

Although he understood that Jesus was his Lord and Savior, “that didn’t necessarily translate to a perfect walk with the Lord,” Michael says. In the late 1990s, however, Michael’s faith grew as he got more involved with his church, and in particular when he actively participated in small groups at the urging of his wife, Cheryl. “I was not thrilled about it,” says Michael. “I am thinking ‘touchy-feely small group sharing emotions’—no, I don’t want to do that. If you want to talk about how I felt when my team lost the Super Bowl, maybe I’ll contribute. But I was wrong. What I experienced in those small groups was quite amazing.”

God’s Will Be Done

After one of those small group meetings in 1999 and when Michael was alone, he prayed a very specific prayer. “I prayed that God’s will would be done in my life,” says Michael. “It was unconditional. It wasn’t the idea that, wow my life will suddenly be perfect, that everything is going to go great in the company. It was that whatever good or bad would come, I wanted God to use me. I would gladly be His servant.”

In retrospect, Michael admits that he did not understand the magnitude of what he was praying. As we will see, his prayer took on special significance beginning in 2001 when his life turned upside down.

Michael's Career

Michael is a serial entrepreneur. The seeds of his opportunistic, risk-taking entrepreneurial drive were planted at age fifteen when he became a competitive freestyle skier. He competed as a skier from his early teens through his early twenties. He also started a ski show company to perform freestyle skiing at events, malls, and convention centers throughout the western U.S. The ski promotion business prospered for several years but was forced to close after a major sponsor—an automobile company—shifted its marketing focus and stopped promoting the ski events. Michael went from success to financial trouble quickly. This financial roller coaster repeats in his life.

Michael describes his life by making an analogy to his days as a competitive freestyle skier. "If you've watched mogul skiing it's amazing with these steep runs with moguls that are sometimes the size of Volkswagens. The challenge is you're supposed to ski down that course as fast as possible." Contestants are judged not only on how fast they can ski, but the quality of their turns and how much air they get going over the jumps. To the viewer, the runs look amazingly smooth. But Michael says, "It is nothing like that.

It is incredibly brutal. The compression on your back and your knees is quite something." To ski well enough to win, you have to push it right to the edge—always being ready to fall and have a disaster. "The reality," he explains, "is that a well-executed run is nothing more than a series of linked recoveries." Michael sees both his career and spiritual life as "a string of linked recoveries."

When the ski promotion business failed, Michael moved out of his apartment and for a few months lived in the back of a semi-trailer. Michael was determined to get his life back together. To make money, he started washing windows and painting houses. His struggle led to a linked recovery.

Michael met a vice president of an electronics distributor while washing his windows and painting his house. The executive hired Michael to sell computer semiconductors for his company. This was Michael's introduction to the electronics business. After several years of success in sales, Michael started his own business manufacturing and distributing memory modules for personal computers and mainframes. The company achieved modest success when such products were hot in the early 1980s. He sold the business to a friend and moved to Silicon Valley.

In Silicon Valley, he worked for other companies in the PC plug-in card business but got burned out. While in the electronics industry, he noticed that technology companies weren't as proficient at marketing as companies in other product sectors. He put his entrepreneurial hat on, yet again. On April 1, 1996, he started a high-technology-focused advertising agency, which he later called H Marketing Services.

H Marketing Services, or "H" as it was called, became one of the fastest growing agencies in the west, reaching over $10 million in annual revenue within its first four years of operations. It focused almost exclusively on high technology clients. In addition to providing traditional marketing services, such as corporate identity, collateral, and advertising, H developed software to provide backend services, such as the processing of leads in real time. Michael found that the software had broader capability than managing the promotional process. It was useful for managing all marketing activities. H invested approximately $10 million to develop the software to broaden its capabilities.

On the Verge of Success When Disaster Strikes

Life was good. Michael lived in a beautiful home, was happily married, had two healthy children—Kaitlin, age 9 and Jack, age 5—and had plenty of money in the bank. And the company was ready to launch its product.

Michael and his team were in New York for the software product launch and had meetings scheduled with over 85 major companies. Its first meeting was on the morning of September 11, 2001, at the top floor of a midtown office building with a clear view of the World Trade Center. As he was finishing up the meeting, Michael watched as the jets flew into the World Trade Center.

"The emotional impact was dramatic," says Michael. The next meeting was scheduled for World Trade Center II. That meeting never happened, and the remaining meetings were canceled. As he and his staff struggled emotionally and had difficulty in making arrangements to return to California, he knew the events of September 11 would be a setback for his business. What he didn't know was how tough it would be.

Marketing budgets disappeared. H was quickly running out of money. He and his firm managed to hunker down and tried their best to keep the company going over the next year. Prayer became an even more important part of Michael's life. "It was a time of desperation and I called on God often to intervene," Michael recalls.

By December of 2002, the company had hit a critical state. The money was gone. His principal funding source, an angel investor, no longer intended to invest. There wasn't much hope for the company. Unexpectedly, however, a sizeable firm came along and expressed interest in acquiring H for the company's technology. After going through the due diligence process with the potential acquirer, Michael determined this was a legitimate opportunity. Any deal, however, was at least three months off. After consulting his wife Cheryl, Michael decided to put their remaining savings into H. Michael now recalls, "This was a bad decision."

He was fully extended financially, but the potential acquisition was moving along. The acquisition would not only solve H's financial problems, but put it in a position to give Michael, his investors, and his employees a healthy return.

The Perfect Storm of Adversity Forms

But in February 2003, Michael encountered another setback. He shared this setback with a small group of trusted, Christian Silicon Valley business leaders that met monthly. The group called itself the Christian President's Group (CPG). It met in a posh conference room at the San Jose Jet Center. I facilitated those meetings. The purpose of the meetings was for members to encourage and help each other to live out their faith in business and at home. Members shared their struggles confidentially and prayed for each other. Group members were well aware of Michael's business and financial difficulties when he shared a major medical issue he was now facing.

"I have a growth in the base of my brain and it's bleeding," Michael stated in a surprisingly matter of fact way. "The doctor tells me that the growth is currently inoperable and it is in a high-rent district of the brain. The growth is called a cavernous malformation in the pons area of the brain atop the brainstem. If I don't have it removed, it is highly likely that I will have a stroke and will die. If they do operate, I am told that paralysis is almost a certainty on one side of my body based upon how they have to go about it."

Years earlier, Michael had gone to Stanford Hospital to find the source of persistent migraine headaches he often experienced. After an MRI, he was told that he had a cavernous malformation in his brain, but that it was small and simply required yearly monitoring. Michael shrugged it off as nothing significant and kept on with his life. But in his exam in February 2003, the doctors noticed that the malformation was growing, had begun bleeding, and posed a major threat to his life. It was fresh from that visit when Michael shared the diagnosis with CPG members.

The five other men with whom Michael was meeting were stunned by his comments. To us, Michael looked like the epitome of health. He was 43 years old, an active golfer, and sported a slight tan. When Michael had shared his news, the men in the CPG group had just finished a discussion about ethics in business and were sharing prayer requests. One of the men asked for God's guidance as he was entangled in a difficult real estate negotiation. Another was struggling financially, and another asked for prayer for his wife who had a minor health problem. These were serious issues, but none had the gravity of the message Michael was delivering.

After a brief period of silence, one colleague asked, "What do you plan to do?"

"For now," Michael answered, "I am going to wait. I am not going to have it removed immediately. We need it to grow to an operable position. I feel fine, except for an occasional headache."

"If the growth gets too large," Michael continued, "I will have to have it removed. If I lose my voice, I can still write. If I become paralyzed, it is likely that I can still work. If I die, I will be home with God. Whatever God has planned for me, I am okay with it."

One colleague asked, "How does your wife feel?"

"Cheryl," Michael replied," was first in shock, but accepts my decision. We plan to go on living, will have the doctors at Stanford Hospital monitor the growth and will trust God for the outcome."

Although Michael felt fine, he faced the real possibility of sudden death. The doctors told him that while they were waiting for the growth to be operable, there was the possibility that it could hemorrhage and he could die. Looking back, Michael offers a stunning view of his circumstances. "Every day I woke up with a very real possibility that it could be my last. That realization really changed my daily interactions." He continues:

> *That is one of the most liberating experiences that a person could have because suddenly what happens is that you get this clarity forced upon you in your life. Every conversation is more important. Every relationship is more valuable. It's just wonderful. It was amazing the depth of the experience. My relationship with others and my relationship with God totally changed. It was the best thing that could have happened to me.*
>
> *And I started to realize is that God had stripped away how I had defined myself. The money was gone – that was my security. Suddenly my security was God, and it was my relationships with others and that was all that mattered and it was wonderful.*

Over the next few months, as the doctors continued to monitor the growth in Michael's brain, the company's prospects took a turn for the worse. The potential acquisition that he hoped would save the company fizzled. Though the company had received a term sheet, the potential acquirer was no longer interested in buying H due to Michael's diagnosis. At the time, Michael's company was barely holding on financially with the money he had put into the company.

Surgery is Necessary

The medical news got worse as well. In September 2003, after Michael began to experience problems swallowing, the doctors who had been monitoring his condition told Michael that the growth had enlarged to take up a majority of the pons area of his brain. They said Michael would be fortunate to make it another week and that surgery was necessary if he hoped to survive. The risks were great. The doctors gave Michael little hope that he could even survive the surgery, and if he did, it was highly likely that he would suffer from severe paralysis. Michael had no choice but to proceed with the operation.

As he prepared for his surgery, people formed groups and networks and started to pray for Michael. He recalls that people would tell him that his faith and the peace and contentment he displayed were inspirational. Michael deflected the comments. "It had nothing to do with me. It wasn't my faith in God; it was God's faith in me. He was there all the time in every moment."

Upon reflection, he admits that prior to adversity he misunderstood scripture. "I thought that my life would always be better and that God would provide for me." He looked at scripture differently now. "What scripture was telling me now was that faith had nothing to do with my financial success; it had nothing to do with my accomplishments; it had everything to do with my soul. And what was important was other people, other relationships."

On October 1, 2003, Michael was in the hospital preparing for surgery. The doctors explained to Michael before the surgery that if he survived he should expect that he would be paralyzed. "As they were rolling me into the O.R., I am thinking there are only three possible outcomes—I am going to die, I am going to be paralyzed, or I'm going to be fine—and I have absolutely no control over which one it's going to be. So it's up to God and, '...whatever You want, God, may Your will be done.' I was okay with that, and the peace and the joy that came over me again goes beyond explanation." Michael says that the medical team in the operating room was so surprised by his apparent joy and contentment that they asked if he had already been given any meds.

During the surgery, a team of neurologists monitored the progress. It was a delicate and dangerous area of the brain in which to operate. Michael was told that the feedback during the surgery was not good. The neurologists expected serious brain damage.

Michael Experiences a Miracle

After the surgery, as Michael was recovering, the neurological team came to his room to see how he was doing. On each of their first four visits, the doctors asked Michael to perform a bicep curl. Michael couldn't do it. On their fifth visit, as they stood at the foot of his bed, one physician asked him again. "Now my vision is all screwed up," says Michael. "I am drugged, and I can barely see anything or understand anything but I move my arm. You would have thought these guys won the lottery. They are screaming and high-fiving and whooping and hollering and running around my room. All I could think is—I guess that's good."

Michael returned to the Stanford Hospital several times after surgery. "The doctors still can't explain what happened," says Michael. My doctors bring in other doctors to meet me. Everybody knows my case. It's fun to be on the receiving end of a miracle."

Interestingly, Michael says that he never prayed for healing for himself. "I simply prayed that God's will be done." But he was on the receiving end of thousands of prayers from others. "It is a very humbling experience," he says. "God obviously answered someone else's prayer because I got all the healing that I ever could have imagined."

A Glimpse of Heaven

Michael received the healing he desired, but also got something more. "There was a moment after surgery," he says, "when I am convinced I got a glimpse of heaven. I can't fully express it, except to say that if you rolled together every wonderful experience in your life—when your children were born, the first time you met your spouse and fell in love—just everything, and you rolled it all together for one moment, and you amplified it by about a hundred times, that is what heaven is. I was overcome with joy and peace and a desire to go home."

For Michael, experiencing heaven created a dilemma. In a conversation I had with Michael weeks after surgery, he says: "It's still a struggle every day. Every day I get up, and there's a little nagging depression in the back of my mind and in my heart that says I want to go home. This is not my home; my home is somewhere else, but God has given me this opportunity to do His work."

For years, Michael says that his wife and children were upset when he would mention his desire to be at home in heaven. He would simply say, "It has nothing to do with how much I love you. It just gets to the core of who we are as followers of Jesus in this fascinating and powerful way."

Michael also experienced a touch of heaven on earth after his surgery. He recalls that when his daughter, Kaitlin, was two years old, she came into his room at night to say, "Daddy, I can't sleep. I'm having bad dreams." Michael walked her back to her room, sat on her bed, talked to her for a minute, kissed her on the forehead, and leaned in close to her ear and whispered, "Sweet dreams, I love you." He kissed her on the cheek and said, "I just gave you enough love to get you through the night and God is in the room watching over you, so please just sleep comfortably."

"Every night after that," Michael says,"Kaitlin asked for a sweet dreams kiss." Even when he traveled, Michael would give Kaitlin a sweet dreams kiss over the phone.

Kaitlin couldn't come to the intensive care room after Michael's surgery, but did see Michael when he was transferred to a standard room. "She came in and just held on to me the whole time. I couldn't really talk and do too much. She is just hanging on to me. When it was finally time to go, she crawled up on the bed and she kissed me on the forehead and said, 'Sweet dreams, I love you.' She kissed me on the cheek, and then said, 'I just gave you enough love to get you through the night and God's in the room watching over you."'

Michael calls the incident "an incredible blessing that comes when we pour out our love to other people and God gives it back to us."

Michael Gets a New Start

Recovery was difficult. And, of course, he couldn't work. With his savings depleted and with the added cost of the surgery he had to declare personal bankruptcy.

It took years before he could think clearly about what he would do next for work. For a period, Michael worked at his church helping with marketing and administrative tasks. But his entrepreneurial desires reemerged. He noticed a need in the market for an entity to facilitate 1031 exchanges in a new, more transparent and secure fashion than the industry norm. A 1031 exchange is a way to defer taxes by buying similar property to one that was sold within a certain period. He also saw a way to apply Silicon Valley technology to the process.

In 2005, he started NES Financial. Today, the company has expanded beyond 1031 exchanges to include other types of financial administration, including facilitating often complex EB-5 alternative capital financing. EB-5 is a U.S. visa category that allows individuals to immigrate to the United States by making investments into approved projects that create U.S. jobs. Using EB-5 investment as a source of alternative capital involves a diverse set of financial, immigration, and job creation requirements that must be clearly and timely documented along with ongoing compliance to a complex level of regulatory requirements. In addition to 1031 and EB-5, NES Financial provides fund administration services to commercial real estate and private equity market sectors.

In 2014, Michael says that NESF managed over $85 billion in 1031 exchanges and by year-end had worked on over 300 EB-5 projects representing aggregate capital raised in excess of $12 billion. NES Financial has been named to the Inc. 5000 fastest-growing private companies in the U.S. multiple times, has received numerous awards for its technology and market leadership, and has three offices around the U.S. and employs around 70 people.

A New Perspective

Twelve years after his surgery, Michael's health is good. He repeats what he said when he initially heard about his medical condition. "I still think it was the best thing that could have happened to me. It made me a different person."

Michael is thankful for what he calls "the amazing work of God"—for healing him and for helping him grow, both emotionally and spiritually. "The only thing that would be better," he says "would be to go home. Life on earth is just different. This isn't my home."

Michael learned that faith is a continual process of growing and experiencing God's blessings and constant presence. "I didn't have the perspective that the surgery was just the start. Now, I see so many ways and so many things that God continues to do. I appreciate that more than ever."

Michael also gained a better appreciation for other people and a desire to help them. He has come alongside friends with prostate cancer and his sister who was diagnosed with Stage 4 aggressive lymphoma. Michael has a different outlook when he sees bad things happen. "Before, when I saw bad things happen, I just saw it as something bad. Today, when I see bad things happen—because I've seen God consistently work in bad things to make some good things—I expect something good to come out of it."

> The biblical concept that Michael expresses about good coming out of bad originates in Romans 8:28: "And we know that God causes everything to work together for the good of those who love God and are called according to his purpose for them." [2] Michael experienced the good news—that God uses "all things" for good for those who trust Him.

Our image of the typical Silicon Valley business person, especially an entrepreneur and CEO, is that of a self-centered individual who drives to succeed, no matter what the obstacle. The image is not that of a person seeking to do the will of God. Yet this is what Michael prayed, what drives Michael today, and what gives him confidence, contentment, and peace in the face of adversity.

Chapter 9
Struggle, Prayer, and Healing

If you are searching for God and do not know where to begin, learn to pray and take the trouble to pray every day... We have to put our trust in Him and love Him, believe in Him, work for Him. And if we pray, we will get the answers we need.[1]
~ Mother Teresa

Kevin Compton

Seven-year-old Kevin and a friend were playing army at a construction site near his home in rural Kansas. The year was 1965. On the site was a framed house sitting on a concrete foundation. The front porch was ready for building; footings were in, and steel rods were sticking out. A pile of sand was close by to mix with cement to make concrete. That day the site was abandoned, as the crew was working at a different location.

With no one there to stop them, the boys couldn't resist climbing on the house and playing in the sand. As Kevin climbed onto one the rafters, he noticed his buddy below. He said to himself, "As he is walking by I can jump down, grapple with him in the sand, and have tons of fun." So Kevin jumped off the house, but missed the guy, and landed on a steel reinforcing rod. The rod entered the back of his leg and traveled up into his intestines, tearing him up.

In great pain and unable to walk on his own, his friend helped Kevin navigate the three blocks to Kevin's home. Seeing the profusion of blood, Kevin's mother rushed young Kevin to the hospital. The attending physician, however, miscalculated the severity of the injury. He saw the wound in the back of Kevin's leg, simply patched it up, and sent Kevin home. That evening the boy's body started to discolor and Kevin was in great pain. His parents rushed him back to the hospital.

A young internist who was on duty properly diagnosed the extent of the injury. "This isn't good," he said. "I don't think there is anything we can do." But Kevin's parents countered, "You operate, we'll pray." The doctor agreed. Kevin's parents found out later that the internist "broke every rule in the hospital," including allowing Kevin to be under anesthesia well beyond what was considered safe at the time. During the long procedure, Kevin's parent's stayed in the waiting area and fervently prayed.

The doctor wasn't optimistic after the operation when he greeted Kevin's parents. "He probably won't live," said the doctor. "If he does, he certainly won't be active—probably won't walk, certainly won't run, will have all sorts of issues. He just won't be normal."

But prayer worked. A miracle happened, and Kevin survived. Not only was he able to walk, but as a teenager he ran the 100-yard dash as a Junior Olympian and even played football.

Today, Kevin Compton is respected among the top venture capitalists in the world. For over twenty years, he helped Silicon Valley's Kleiner Perkins Caufield & Byers earn hundreds of millions of dollars for its investors. The firm invested in such high-flying companies as Amazon, Google, Electronic Arts, Netscape, Intuit and many others.

His career also includes a role as an active owner of the San Jose Sharks professional hockey team. In 2013, Kevin left Kleiner Perkins to cofound a venture fund called Radar Partners, which invests in early-stage technology companies. In addition, he and his wife are engaged in microfinancing projects in depressed areas in Third World countries.

Why Was His Life Spared?

Thoughts of his near-death experience, however, still linger in Kevin's mind. "Why was my life spared? Why do I have this great story to tell? I was spared for a reason."

Was his life spared to help fund and launch many innovative businesses, and to give him a platform to tell his story and influence others for Christ? He has had many opportunities to do just that, including talks at the National Prayer Breakfast, Christian forums, and several community prayer breakfasts, including the one in Silicon Valley. When Kevin speaks publicly, he freely passes on the wisdom he has learned in business and as a man of God.

Thousands of people have heard Kevin list his "Five Rules for Success."

- **Live by the golden rule.** – "Treat others as you want to be treated" as expressed in the Bible in Matthew 7:12. "If you put this rule in practice for just a few weeks, it becomes a habit to live by."
- **Have a sense of urgency.** – "I work hard to make very few lists. If possible, I take care of things right away. Sometimes I will stop in the middle of a meeting and say, 'Let's just fix this now.' If you work hard to get things done right away, people will appreciate it. They will realize that their need is a priority for you."
- **Make an effort, knowing that results will vary.** – "It's better to make an effort than only trying when you know you won't fail or waiting until everything is right."
- **Think big.** – Compton believes you accomplish little unless you have big dreams and act on those dreams.
- **Think small.** – "The difference between success and mediocrity is attention to detail. I try to honor my schedule. When things are supposed to start on time, I try to be there. When things are supposed to happen, I try to be a part of them." Kevin begins every day by reflecting on the previous day and often writes handwritten notes to thank or encourage people.

For what reason was he healed? Throughout his career, he has stayed connected with the community and his church. For over fifteen years, he has taught adult Sunday school classes that have had as many as 150 attendees. He is on the board of Transforming the Bay Area with Christ (TBC), as referred to previously, a coalition of business and faith leaders formed to make a difference in the Bay Area. Kevin also has a passion for youth and sports. For several years, he coached Pop Warner football and helped out as an assistant coach at a local Silicon Valley football powerhouse, Valley Christian High School. Was his life spared to lead church and community activities and to guide young people?

Perhaps Kevin was healed at a young age for all these reasons. Due both to his success and his story of how God has worked through him, he speaks with authority and conviction. At the same time, Kevin is humble, even soft-spoken. Kevin Compton is a man of God who lives a life of service and integrity. He also has a good sense of humor. When I asked him about his personal commitment to Christ, he remarked:

The Purpose of Suffering

One of the mysteries of Christian faith is that we don't know why some people suffer much and some little; some die at a young age and some don't. Followers of Christ, however, take comfort in knowing that we have an all-powerful God who has a plan that we do not always know.[2]

> *I was saved at seven, nine, eleven, fourteen, twenty-three, twenty-eight, and about two weeks ago. But in high school is when Christ became much more personal to me. I never doubted God or Jesus, but questioned myself—my ability to be a good*

Christian. Am I living up to my potential? Am I living up to my obligations? Am I a good witness? I've not been one of the ones who blame God when things go wrong. I look at myself.

Prayer and healing at a young age strongly influenced not only Kevin Compton's life, but the many people he leads in business, in his church, and in his community.

Dustin Keele and Jaida Im also experienced relief from suffering through prayer.

Dustin Keele

Dustin Keele is a Silicon Valley entrepreneur. He and his wife, Christine, live in a remote mountain ranch house in the South Bay. For years, they have provided financial support for two children in Ethiopia through Compassion International, a faith-based nonprofit organization. In August 2013, the Keeles had the opportunity to travel to Ethiopia to meet the children they support and to serve the local community on a trip sponsored by their church and Compassion. Dustin was hesitant to go because he was in the midst of working on a $2.5 billion solar proposal that was due while he was scheduled to be on the trip. But a few months before the trip, Dustin had a dream.

In the dream, I had returned from a trip to Ethiopia. I was in a room talking with a broken man about Jesus. There was something different in the way I

> *felt within the dream. There was a new depth in my relationship with God. When I woke up, I knew that I had to go on this trip. I told my wife, "I have to go to Ethiopia. I hope that we can go together, but I know that I have to go."*
>
> *I had a sense that God was going to do something on the mission trip that would profoundly change my life and somehow add new depth to my relationship with Him, which I already felt was deep.*

Life in Ethiopia Impacts Dustin

The visit to Ethiopia impacted Dustin in two ways. He was profoundly affected "by seeing things outside the bubble in which we live." Poverty is pervasive. The mother of one of the children who Dustin and Christine sponsor earns the equivalent of only $20 per month. With the rent costing $10 per month, there was little money for things other than food prior to funding the family receives from Compassion. Dustin says that without funding from Compassion, "the children would just fend for themselves all day and play in the dirt. They would have no hope." The Compassion funding and associated programs changed that. The children are now in school, receiving proper medical care, and are on course to break the cycle of poverty.

Dustin notes that people in the village take their Christian faith seriously. Worship services are typically three hours long. "People don't worship like we worship," says

Dustin. "They're passionate. It's half singing and dancing, and half preaching—and all energy."

Miracles

Prior to the trip, Dustin had heard that miracles were happening in Africa, and he hoped to see some for himself. Dustin remarks amusingly, "I specifically wanted to see somebody with a shriveled arm reach out and miraculously have a healthy one." Dustin did not see a shriveled arm healed in front of him, but unexpectedly did experience a miracle himself.

While in Ethiopia, Dustin awakened one morning at 3:30 a.m. He opened his Bible and read 1 Corinthians, Chapter 12 which describes the physical manifestations of the Holy Spirit, one of which is healing. Dustin told his wife, "Honey, I think somebody with the gift of healing is going to pray for us."

After a three-hour Friday night worship service at which he witnessed a woman prayed over and healed of an evil spirit, Dustin decided to talk to the preacher, an Ethiopian man named Alebachew. As he was approaching Alebachew, Dustin was surprised to see Alebachew point at him and say, "You, I am supposed to pray for you." Alebachew asked Dustin if he had any physical ailments that needed healing. Dustin told the preacher he had severe acid reflux. Dustin had battled acid reflux for years and was taking prescription medicine to ease the symptoms. While in Ethiopia, Dustin's acid reflux had gotten worse primarily due to the strong coffee he was drinking. It is a tradition in Ethiopia to drink strongly brewed coffee during social occasions.

Dustin describes Alebachew's prayer this way:

> *So he starts praying over me in a blend of English and Amharic. He then slips into tongues, which is really strange for somebody from the Bay Area. You don't hear a whole lot of speaking in tongues at the churches in the Silicon Valley. As he is praying for me, I feel this general warmth and tingling sensation over my body, which is something that I've experienced before in times of prayer. However, there is no specific sensation in the area of my stomach where the acid reflux was.*

By the next morning, however, Dustin's acid reflux was gone. He was able to stop taking his medicine, and even continued to drink coffee with no acid reflux symptoms. As of this writing—nearly two years after this experience—Dustin is still free of acid reflux. He is taking no medication and still is happily drinking coffee.

Perhaps like me, you are skeptical when you hear stories like this. But I know Dustin as a friend and can attest to his healing.

A Vision for Dustin

As a final note to Dustin's story, the preacher who prayed over him that Friday night commented to Dustin after his prayer:

> *You know God doesn't always give me a vision for people. But while I was praying for you, I had a vision. In the vision, you were holding a white piece of paper in your hands. The piece of paper turned to ash. God is giving you a new piece of paper. The new piece of paper means that you're going to be doing something new with your life. In addition, God is giving you a key, and the key is to unlock something that he wants to give you.*

Dustin is on a search to find out what that "something new" is.

Why did Dustin experience a sudden cure, what he calls a miracle? Dustin believes that one reason is that he can now give testimony to God's power. At a talk he gave at the Stanford Faculty Club in 2014, he said this:

> *I feel like the reason God had this trip happen, and the reason He's brought me back to the Bay Area is to share this. To let you know that the God that we follow and the God that we believe in is real. He is still at work. All of these miracles didn't stop at Pentecost.*

Pentecost

Pentecost is a Jewish celebration 50 days after Passover. Acts Chapter 2 describes the coming of the Holy Spirit to the disciples as they gathered together to celebrate Pentecost.

Most Christians think of this event as the birth of the Church.[3]

Jaida Im

In October 2008, Jaida Im was in despair. Due to severe migraines, she was forced to take a leave of absence from a job she loved with Kaiser. Jaida had suffered from severe migraines for years. She tried everything medically available. Nothing worked. She was at the point of taking her life.

Today, she is a vibrant person helping transform the lives of women rescued from human trafficking. She suffers from no migraines and is taking no medication to prevent them.

What happened to cause this radical change in her life? Let's take a look.

Faith and Career

As a young girl growing up in South Korea, Jaida attended Buddhist temples and watched her mother pray to the Buddha. At age ten, she moved with her family to the U.S., and was introduced to Christianity through junior high school friends. Her curiosity with Christian faith grew out of the peace she felt at church and the friendliness of the people she met. Both her parents were busy making a living as pharmacists and did not express concern with Jaida's interest in Christianity.

In college at the University of California, Santa Barbara (UCSB), she met her future husband, Karl, who was a devout Christian. They married after they finished their first year of schooling. Upon graduation from UCSB with a degree in engineering, Karl went to work for Hughes Aircraft. Jaida decided to follow in her parents' footsteps by becoming a pharmacist. She attended graduate school in pharmacy studies at the University of Southern California (USC).

For a period, her marriage struggled. Among other issues, Jaida felt inadequate in her faith compared to Karl. He led various activities at their church, including Bible studies. Karl suggested she join him at a church he was attending. "Amazingly," says Jaida, "that is what brought us back together—the church and the people praying for us. I knew that God wanted us to get back together."

Upon graduation from USC, Jaida landed a "dream job" at Kaiser in southern California. She worked as an ambulatory care clinical pharmacist developing a program for respiratory care patients with asthma, emphysema, and other breathing conditions. She loved her job and was successful. Through her work, emergency room visits decreased, the quality of life for patients improved, and costs from the hospital went down.

Career was Jaida's priority. Faith was secondary.

A History of Medical Problems

For much of her life, Jaida suffered from physical issues. She refers to herself as a weakling. Motion sickness was common—something that she found out later was a precursor to migraine headaches people experience as adults. She also suffered from GI (gastrointestinal) problems.

It was not until 1997, however, at the age of 35 that her migraines grew more frequent and more severe. She had an MRI, a CAT scan, and many consultations with doctors. There was no tumor and nothing else physically identifiable as the cause. On her doctor's advice, she experimented with a variety of drugs over the next several years, but did not find relief.

From 1997 to 2008, her career grew but her medical condition never abated. Everything triggered her migraines—lights, noise, eating, and travel. "I would wake up crying. I had this throbbing pain behind my eyes. I was often dizzy, and my mind was fogged up." Jaida even tried Eastern medicine—acupuncture and acupressure—but nothing eased the pain. Jaida first transferred to a part-time schedule, but she soon had to take a medical leave of absence from her job.

With her career—and identity—gone, she fell into a period of depression. Although faith was secondary, she hoped that prayer would work to relieve her suffering. But God did not seem to answer her prayers.

The pain came frequently and with more intensity. Jaida questioned her sister who had married a pastor. "If God is a

God of love, why do I have to suffer? Why isn't He taking care of me if He loves me?" She received no answers. Prayer didn't work, and drugs didn't work.

"I never knew how excruciating life could be. How unenjoyable. There was no hope. I said to myself, 'Okay, I am just going to take my life.'"

Jaida shared her suicidal tendencies with her husband and close friends. They were very concerned and tried to help, but Jaida found no comfort and relief. Then a new friend came into her life—someone who Jaida now calls "a very special friend." Her name was Janelle. Janelle was a devout Christian who prayed often for Jaida.

In early October 2008, Janelle called Jaida. "I know you are feeling miserable, and I know it is hard for you to get out, but there is a pastor from Korea coming to the Jubilee Christian Center. I am performing with a group of women. It is a special event, please come."

Because she trusted Janelle, Jaida decided to attend, and mustered enough strength to drive on her own. Jubilee is a megachurch that sits on a multi-acre campus located on the fringe of industrial parks housing high-tech companies in San Jose. Jubilee is non-denominational and charismatic in orientation.

The church was packed when Jaida arrived—perhaps more than 2,000 people in attendance. The usher asked if Jaida was alone. When she answered "Yes," she was ushered to the front, just four or five rows from the altar. As she looked at the program, she realized that she had never heard of the guest speaker that night. She now knows he was

Yongi Cho, a pastor of a huge church in South Korea, one of the world's largest. Pastor Cho periodically travels to conduct healing ceremonies.

"He spoke a simple sermon, but as I sat there listening, I stared at him. I could see his face and he seemed to be staring at me." Jaida felt something come over her, which in retrospect she believes was a message from God. She had a sense that she needed to ask Pastor Cho to pray for her. After the service, however, Jaida was disappointed that the ushers did not allow people to approach Pastor Cho. He was in his seventies and frail. "I guess they didn't want people stomping over him and grabbing him."

When Janelle rejoined Jaida after the service, however, she told Jaida that she knew Pastor Cho from old family ties. She told Jaida that Jaida was invited to join her for lunch with Pastor Cho. When they got to the room with Pastor Cho, he was surrounded by guards. Janelle approached Pastor Cho and told him about Jaida and her condition and asked if he would pray for her. "I would be honored to do so," he told Janelle.

Jaida got down on her knees and Pastor Cho put his hands on Jaida's head and prayed for healing. She remarks, "I did not feel anything at the moment but accepted the prayer. When I got home, I prayed to God, 'I accept that You are going to heal me, or I am going to die.' That night I stopped all medication. Either I would be healed or I would die. This is the end of the road."

That night Jaida's body began to purge itself. She remarks, "It was a cleansing time for me. My son wanted to call 911, but I felt I wasn't dying. I realized that this was something I had to go through." The purging stopped after the third day. On the fourth day, Jaida rested from exhaustion. "When I woke up," she says, "I was a new person. My mind was crystal clear. I was as light as a feather. I felt like I could fly. I knew I was healed and started praising God. Even my husband commented that I looked and sounded different. I was a new creation, full of energy and life."

Jaida found that she had no more headaches. The things that previously would bring on the migraines—light, noise, certain food, and so on—did not bother her anymore. She realized that she had been given a second chance at life. She began praying about what to do about work, and she was convinced to give up her career as a pharmacist, which had been a stronghold for her and got in the way of her relationship with God.

But what was next for Jaida? "I wanted to serve God and was willing to do whatever he wanted me to do." As she surrendered her life to God, she also began the search for what was next.

God Uses Adversity for Good

People vary in their reactions to personal struggle and adversity. Some grow bitter and blame others and God for their circumstances. Suffering seems unfair when others we know are flourishing—especially those who lack integrity, are self-absorbed, and mistreat others for their personal gain.

But, as with Jaida, God is available to intervene and rescue people from despair, if they are open to listening to Him.

Some people maintain an attitude of hope through their pain; they expect that at some point good will come out of struggle. They grow closer to God, deepen their character, gain humility, develop empathy for others who suffer similarly, and may even want to help people suffering in a similar fashion.

> Having an attitude of hope in the midst of struggle is what the Bible teaches.

Having an attitude of hope in the midst of suffering is what the Bible teaches. In Romans, Chapter 8, we read: "...we also glory in our sufferings, because we know that suffering produces perseverance; perseverance, character; and character, hope. And hope does not put us to shame, because God's love has been poured out into our hearts through the Holy Spirit, who has been given to us."[4] And as noted in Chapter 8 of Romans, God works for good for those who love Him.[5]

Good came out of the struggles for Kevin Compton and Dustin Keele, and as we will see, for Jaida Im. Prayer was a key element. Each had a similar reaction: "For what purpose was I healed?" Their faith grew deeper, as did their reliance on God. Kevin still contemplates the reason why his life was spared. Dustin is searching for the reason God healed him in such a dramatic fashion. In Chapter 10 you will read the rest of Jaida's story—how God called her to a new profession.

10
Pain and Purpose

God's purpose is greater than our problem, our pain, and even our sin.[1]
~ Rick Warren

When Jaida Im was cured from her debilitating migraine headaches, she realized that she had been given a second chance at life. She prayed for guidance for what God wanted her to do next. Should she go back to work as a pharmacist or do something else? Since her work as a pharmacist was a stronghold that got in the way of her relationship with God, she rejected that idea. But what should she do?

She decided to take the time to see how God would lead her. Although she was initially concerned about finances, she says, "God gave me peace. He is an awesome God. He gave me a new life—a miracle, and would lead me to a new career."

For much of her adult life, Jaida had a heart for women, especially those impoverished. Possibly that was a direction God wanted her follow. In October 2008, she and her husband, Karl, joined a church—Abundant Life Christian Fellowship. She met with a counselor who suggested that Jaida look into areas that matched her desires and talents. The counselor made two recommendations: to consider helping homeless women, and to join the church's Global

Ministry Team. Jaida also started volunteering at a teen pregnancy center.

At her first Global Ministry Team meeting, she heard a presentation about human trafficking and sex slavery in the Bay Area. Jaida was dumfounded that such evil practices were happening so close to home. She began to research the problem, including reading *Not for Sale* by David Batstone,[2] in which Batstone discusses his personal exposure to trafficking in the Bay Area and the problem in the U.S. and around the world. "At the same time," Jaida says, "God started putting thoughts in my head about a shelter for women." She wasn't sure what population of women to serve but had a sense that God wanted her to open a shelter of some sort for women in need.

Jaida Finds a New Calling

In February 2009, Jaida attended an anti-trafficking conference. During one presentation, the speaker commented, "There is no home in the Bay Area for survivors of human trafficking due to the risk and expense." God put a a strong leaning in Jaida's heart when she heard that statement. Immediately, she knew that she had found her calling.

But how should she proceed? She knew a shelter would require a big financial commitment. She also knew little about anti-trafficking issues and even less about opening a shelter and running a ministry. But she was leaning on God for direction. And she needed to make sure Karl was in agreement with the direction she sensed from God.

Karl was skeptical at first and agreed to pray about the decision. Karl received confirmation from God, when, after praying, he came across the book *Tipping Point*.[3] He sensed that the shelter and ministry he and Jaida contemplated opening could help "tip" the problem of human trafficking in the Bay Area in a more positive direction. Armed with a new sense of purpose and direction, Jaida embarked on the journey to open a home and a ministry. "I had so much faith in God and trusted that this is what He wants. I knew that He would be the provider, not me."

God does what we cannot do, but we do what we can do. Jaida started on what she could do, relying on God in the process. She found an attorney to set up a nonprofit organization called "Freedom House." She asked friends and family for financial support and started looking for homes and agencies with which Freedom House could partner. Of particular help was an attorney who had set up a similar home in India.

> God does what we cannot do, but we do what we can do.

Money was the key issue. 2009 was not a good year for the U.S. economy and most people, including Karl and Jaida. The money they had was tied up as collateral for a bank loan for Karl's business that they could not access for three years. Through what Jaida calls "a miracle," the bank made an exception and let them access the funds. Jaida and

Karl then had enough money for a down payment and to renovate what Jaida calls an "ideal" home they had found.

As the renovations proceeded over the next several months, Jaida secured partnerships with law enforcement and community service organizations and hired staff. Everything came together. Jaida and her staff opened the home in August 2010. They named it "The Monarch."

The Monarch provides aftercare for up to eight adult women at a time. The women survivors receive counseling, support, legal and vocational help, and medical treatment. The expected stay at the home is typically no more than 18 months, after which the women engage in everyday life in the community. Some go on to get a degree. Others start a career.

"Freedom House is a place I thought no longer existed in this world," says a survivor of human trafficking. "When I was forced to become a prostitute, I saw the ugly my family warned me of, and I believed that the world no longer possessed good. This is a home that the staff has worked so hard to create for women like me to feel safe and see what beauty God has to give. I have learned so much living here. I have learned how to empower myself, to stand tall and strong for myself."

Jaida also noticed that there was a need to serve younger victims of human trafficking—girls 12 to 17 years old. She committed Freedom House to open a second residence. In early 2014, Freedom House opened a shelter it called "Nest" that serves up to six girls at a time while providing referral and support services to non-resident survivors similar to those at The Monarch.

The two shelters and associated ministries are transforming the lives of hundreds of human trafficking victims. Their lives may not have been restored if Jaida had not suffered from the pain she did and responded to God's leading. Pain led Jaida to an intimate relationship with God and a new calling. "Giving hope and restoration" is how Jaida now describes her life mission. She gained even more. "My life, my marriage, everything was restored and made new. All the honor goes to the Lord for what He designed, including the things I had to go through to become who I am now."

No one avoids a life of pain and adversity. We are either in the midst of it, affected by past struggle, or about to experience it. What matters is what we do about it. Jaida was on the verge of suicide before God touched her life both to cure her and to give her a calling that is giving life to others.

Tess Reynolds was living a life most of us long for—business success and a happy family. Tragedy, however, interrupted her life. Like Jaida, adversity brought her closer to God, and God used Tess's tragedy to give hope and opportunity to others.

Tess Reynolds

Tess Reynolds is an engaging woman with jet-black hair and olive-colored skin that derives from her Philippine heritage. She serves as the CEO of New Door Ventures, a thriving nonprofit organization having a major impact on disadvantaged youth ages 16 to 21 in San Francisco. Helping the disadvantaged, however, was not how Tess envisioned her career when she graduated with an MBA from Santa Clara University. She was on a fast track first in brand management and then in high technology before experiencing personal tragedy. Guidance from God caused her to change her priorities and career. She found a new purpose and calling.

Tess's Business Career

While in the Philippines, Tess launched her career with Procter & Gamble, the king of brand management. Next, a manager lured her away to Coca-Cola. After moving to the U.S. to join her family and attend business school, she landed in Silicon Valley and fell in love with the emerging personal computing industry—and her soon-to-be-husband, Tim. In 1985, Tess joined Software Publishing Corporation, one of the pioneers of the software industry, where she co-created the first presentation graphics program, Harvard Graphics. The product was a quick hit, and Tess became the business unit general manager.

In spite of her obvious life-long success, however, Reynolds did not feel fulfilled. "I pressured myself to be 'somebody' in the world. Because graduate schools cared about GPAs (grade point averages) and GMATs (Graduate Management Admission Tests), I did, too. I took a job at Procter & Gamble probably because it was one of the most difficult places to get a job. I learned the art of moving up and did quite well. While still in my 20s, I was managing over 200 people. Accomplishments are fine, but I had a problem. The more of a somebody I became in the world, the more I lost track of who I was."

A setback caused her to reconsider her priorities. In her 30s, Tess experienced a devastating second-trimester miscarriage. A card she received during this time got her attention. It read, "I lift up my eyes to the hills—where does my help come from? My help comes from the Lord, the Maker of Heaven and Earth." Those words from Psalm 121 helped her realize that up to this point her first source of help had not been God. She relied on her skills, hard work, and connections.

Although Tess was a follower of Christ her whole life, faith was not her priority at that time. The grief she experienced from her miscarriage caused her turn to God. "I ran out of options, and my system wasn't working. I admitted that the life I wanted wasn't the life I was living, so I began making changes." She joined a Bible study and a small group of working women who struggled with balancing faith and family. Over the next few years, her faith came alive, and the Bible became a practical guide to her life.

She also had two children—first Chris, and then Matthew.

Her deepening spiritual life helped her understand that her work and travel schedule were getting in the way of living more fully with God and her family. She mustered the courage to leave her lucrative corporate job to start a consulting practice, even if it meant financial uncertainty.

Unexpectedly, success came again. She garnered an enviable list of high-tech clients, including Adobe, AMD, Hewlett-Packard, and IBM as well as venture-funded technology companies.

A Personal Tragedy

Five years into running her consulting business, she experienced a life-changing event that no one wants to experience. In July 1998, her 6-year-old son, Matthew, came home from basketball camp with a limp. Tess was concerned but did not expect the diagnosis. Matthew had bone cancer.

Devastated but diligent, Tess and her husband sought a solution. Unfortunately, to arrest the cancer, Matthew needed to have his leg amputated, and required rigorous chemotherapy. Tess and her husband agreed to the amputation and shuttled Matthew to the hospital for treatment over the next thirteen months. It was a difficult time for Tess and her family, but as the treatments ended, they were optimistic that Matthew was cured.

The family's hopefulness was crushed, however, when five months later they found out that cancer had come back aggressively. Matthew had to endure more surgery, chemotherapy, and even experimental drugs. Tess wrestled with God during this period. "How could God allow an innocent child to suffer so much?"

Tess bonded with the other mothers of children at the hospital who shared similar experiences. "I can't even begin to list all the horrible things that happened to our children." They asked, "What if the stories in the Bible are just myths? What if there is no heaven?"

"I had fear, anger, and pain," says Tess. "So did my family. Psychotherapy helped, but in the end I found that there was no place to turn but to God. I scoured the pages of scripture for answers. Nowhere did I find God promising to exempt His followers from pain and suffering. What I did find was His promise never to leave or forsake me, His promise that nothing could separate me from His love—not death or cancer—and His promise that His grace would be sufficient for me. And indeed, His grace was generously sufficient."

Matthew's Love for God Inspires Tess

The trauma of her child in pain, as well as the bravery and faith he exhibited, drove Tess to what she calls "a more intimate" relationship with Christ. As Tess reflects on Matthew's life, she sees that God was with Matthew from the time he was created, and had prepared him for his battle with cancer. From a very young age, it was clear that Matthew loved God. At age four for example, when the family was discussing what to have for Christmas dinner, Matthew suggested five loaves of bread and two fish "because that was Jesus's favorite food." From that day forward, bread and fish became part of the Reynolds family Christmas meal.

One depressingly rainy day when Tess was driving Matthew home from the hospital, the sun briefly appeared. Matthew immediately yelled, "Praise God for the sunshine!" Tess opened the sunroof of her car. "It was such a happy moment. We began to sing, and Matthew was sort of dancing in his seat as we enjoyed the sunshine." Tess came to call such moments "smooches from God."

Matthew's second grade class presented him with a beautiful quilt his teacher and classmates had made. The quilt had drawings of what were special to Matthew, including swimming and street hockey, puppies and Pokemon. Matthew's eyes focused, however, on what was in the corner of the quilt. He burst out, "Thank you for the cross!"

Matthew's love of God and intimacy with Him profoundly affected Tess. That is why she calls Matthew's cancer years both "the worst and the sweetest" of her life.

Matthew died in August of 2000 at the age of 8. Before he died, Matthew passed along to his family a special experience. "In his final hours," remembers Tess,

God Is Always with Us

As we go through difficulty, it is common to feel that God has abandoned us. We ask why God hasn't answered our prayers. The consolation for followers of Christ is that "God's ways are not our ways"[4] and that He is with us always. God has a larger plan that we cannot see. The Bible is replete with references to God's love for us and the promise that He is with us always, especially in times of trouble.[5]

"Matthew spoke of heaven and angels singing the Hallelujah Chorus. There is no doubt in my mind that heaven exists and that is where my son is and where I am going."

Discerning God's Will

Following Matthew's death, Tess felt restless about her work. "The cancer world was both high-tech and high touch," she says, "but my consulting practice was just high-tech. I longed for a way to impact people more than with products and profits."

Tess began a long process of praying and trying to discern what God wanted her to do next. Two years later, she received a call from a recruiter asking her to consider the CEO position of an organization called Golden Gate Community, which was later renamed New Door Ventures. It served disadvantaged people in San Francisco through jobs, training, and personal support.

After much deliberation, Tess took the job in 2003. "This was a huge career change, but it seemed like a clear call from God. I left the business world to work in a ministry that is also a business. Today we run two businesses and partner with over 50 other organizations to serve as job training centers for disconnected youth."

New Door Ventures

The young people who New Door serves come out of challenging circumstances. "These are not the people who would make the top of any hiring list," says Tess. Most have histories of homelessness, foster care, crime, or use of drugs and alcohol. Many have experienced some form of trauma, and all live below poverty level. She recalls one young man who took 17 bullets that were meant for his drug-dealing father, but survived.

New Door helps prepare these young people for work and life through paid job internships, skill-building workshops, educational support, and most importantly, individual support. The last ingredient Tess says is the "secret sauce." Over 90% of their graduates move on to regular jobs, further education or both. Nearly all the youth with criminal backgrounds do not reoffend, and over 90% remain in stable housing when checked at New Door's six month follow-up. Since Tess joined New Door, more than one-thousand youth have graduated from their programs.

"God has been visibly at work in powerful ways," Tess reflects. "He has done more than we could ever ask or imagine."

New Door Ventures is the proud recipient of several awards, including the Bank of America Neighborhood Builder's Award, granted to only two nonprofits in the San Francisco region annually. In 2014, New Door purchased and moved into a 14,000-square-foot building to accommodate plans to provide 2,000 jobs for youth over the next decade. The future looks bright both for New Door and for Tess.

"I am excited about the future," she says. "I have gained so much by helping others grow." She also gained something more. Through the emotional pain she experienced from a second-trimester miscarriage and the loss of a child to cancer, she established an even deeper relationship with God and a new purpose for her life.

Through adversity and pain, Reggie Littlejohn also found a deeper relationship with God and a new purpose.

Reggie Littlejohn—A Woman on a Mission

Reggie Littlejohn has led four lives—from atheist to believer, from litigator to international rights advocate, from a person with boundless energy to a bedridden patient for five years, then back again to an energetic world traveler, nonprofit leader, and public speaker. She views it all as part of God's plan to shed light on abuses done to women and girls worldwide, especially in China. She is outspoken, intense, and passionate about her work. At a young age she exhibited such characteristics.

From Atheist to Believer

Reggie grew up in a Christian home, but at age sixteen announced to her parents that she was an atheist and refused to go to church. Her faith journey moved from atheist to agnostic when she read the Bible for the first time in an ancient literature course in college. "As I read the Gospel of John, I realized just who this person Jesus was and what he did. I told myself, 'This is not what I rejected.'"

She married her college sweetheart, Robert. Following graduation, Reggie enrolled at Yale Law School, while her husband attended Yale Divinity School. She took a year off from her studies to travel around the world. On two separate trips, Reggie had the opportunity to meet Mother Teresa and volunteer with Mother Teresa's Missionaries of Charity in Calcutta. She spent mornings in Mass and evenings at a "Holy Hour." "Mother Teresa was repeatedly reaching out to me," says Reggie. Reggie spent days ministering either to the people who were dying or people in tremendous need. "By the end of this, I totally believed in God."

Following law school, Reggie gave birth to her son, Nico. She decided to wait a year before taking a job at a law firm in San Francisco to care for her newborn. During her time off, she audited classes at the Yale Divinity School, where Robert was attending. "It was the first time I ever read the entire New Testament. The whole message just blew me away. By the end of that I was a committed Christian."

Reggie Launches Her Career as a Litigator

After law school, Reggie and Robert headed to San Francisco where she took a position as a litigation associate in a major law firm. She planned to stay at the firm only until her student loan was paid off but found that she loved her work as a litigator. During her eight-year stint as a litigator, she performed pro bono work, helping Chinese refugees seeking asylum in the United States.

Reggie's first refugee was a woman who had been persecuted as a Christian and forcibly sterilized. "That opened two whole worlds up to me," says Reggie. "First, I didn't know that Christians were persecuted in China. Second, I knew that China had a one-child policy, but I never stopped to think how it was enforced. I did not realize until I represented this woman that it was enforced through forced abortion, forced sterilization, and infanticide. I was utterly appalled."

Adversity Changes Her Thinking

During her years as a lawyer, Reggie became pregnant with her second child. Sadly, this pregnancy ended in a miscarriage. Reggie was heartbroken. She called her mother. "Why would God allow me to get pregnant with a child that would be so loved and so well cared for, and then take that child away?" Her mother answered, "We may never be able to answer that question, but I believe that somehow, God will use this pain for a purpose."

Reggie now believes that the pain of her miscarriage and a second miscarriage she experienced a short time later sensitized her to the suffering of women losing babies against their will. "Of course, I have never suffered the violence of a forced abortion. But I do know what it's like to lose two babies that I wanted. I believe that, because of the painful loss of my own babies through miscarriage, when I heard that women are forcibly aborted in China, my response was visceral. I just couldn't look the other way."

Then Reggie experienced another setback. In 2003, she developed multiple breast lumps. Because of her strong family history of breast cancer, she had bilateral mastectomies with implant reconstruction. Unfortunately, during the surgery she contracted an MRSA staph infection, which is often deadly. She left the practice of law on a medical leave of absence and was disabled for five years. During that five-year period, Reggie had to undergo several surgeries. She developed chronic fatigue syndrome as well. Her time as a patient, however, became a spiritual awakening.

"I cast myself on the Lord and He gave me this hunger for His Word. I read the Bible over and over. The Bible says, 'Do not be conformed to this world, but be transformed by the renewing of your mind.'[6] I felt that the Lord was renewing my mind."

During convalescence, her thoughts turned to the women suffering in China. "I felt called to begin praying for those worse off than I was. I began to pray for Christians who were being tortured for their faith and women whose pregnancies were being forcibly aborted. It became my sole focus and consuming passion to do something about this abuse."

Reggie Finds a New Purpose

"My mission went from making lots of money as an attorney to helping women and babies devastated by forced abortion and female gendercide in China due to China's

One-Child Policy." Reggie researched the unintended consequences of China's One-Child Policy—forced abortion, forced sterilization, death from botched procedures—and the situation where there are 37 million more men than women living in China. The distorted ratio of men to women results in human trafficking and sexual slavery, which in turn is a cause for the high rate of female suicide.

By the end of 2008, Reggie started feeling better. With renewed energy, she founded the nonprofit organization, Women's Rights Without Frontiers (WRWF), which has been called the leading voice to expose and oppose forced abortion, gendercide, and sexual slavery in China.

As WRWF's leader, Reggie has had the opportunity to speak many times on the *Voice of America*, the U.S. official broadcast into China, Taiwan, and Hong Kong. She has spoken before the European Parliament, the British and Irish Parliaments, and at universities, including Harvard and Stanford law schools. She has briefed officials at the White House, the U.S. State Department, the United Nations, and the Vatican. Also, she has testified seven times before the U.S. Congress.

She has had many television and radio appearances, including CNN, C-Span, and Voice of America. In January, 2013, Reggie was given the National Pro-Life Recognition Award at the 40th Annual March for Life. Her vision is to draw pro-life and pro-choice advocates together to fight forced abortion. As she says, "Forced abortion is not a choice." In addition, she is engaged in the "Save a Girl" campaign that has saved hundreds of baby girls from sex-selected abortion, abandonment, or grinding poverty in China.

Inside the Vatican Magazine recognized Reggie as one of its "Top Ten" people in the world for 2013. The magazine chooses people "whose witness can instruct and inspire us."[7]

Her private life reflects her public advocacy. In 2013, she rescued two girls from China when their father, pro-democracy hero, Zhang Lin, was jailed. Reggie and her husband are now raising the girls as their own daughters. Reggie says, "I feel God is healing me from the pain of my two miscarriages by giving me two beautiful daughters from China."

As she looks back, Reggie sees how God's plan took shape in her life. "I see it all as part of God's plan for me—Mother Teresa, my illness, the opportunity to represent Chinese refugees as a lawyer, and even my miscarriages. If I had not lost my own babies in miscarriage, I might not have developed the passion for helping women who were victims of forced abortion."

The faith journeys of Jaida Im, Tess Reynolds, and Reggie Littlejohn, though different, reflect a similar theme. Each experienced pain and adversity but grew closer to God as a result, and each found new purpose. When tragedy and pain strike, we can get angry with God (often our first reaction), or we can run to God where we find comfort, a deep and lasting relationship, and often a new purpose.

Four:
A Higher Calling

God providentially weaves the threads of His Call through our lives…[1]
~ Oswald Chambers

What is your calling? Have you ever given much thought to your calling? Most people think of calling as a vocational or career path they feel equipped and passionate about following. In the Roman Catholic tradition and other Christian traditions, calling is often associated with discerning a vocation as a priest or minister. Calling is sometimes associated with a passion for serving the needs of the poor or disadvantaged. But calling has meaning beyond a vocation or avocation. Calling is also a request or demand that requires a response, as when a boss calls a subordinate into his office. Calling also refers to names and titles people are given. For example, we still call former U.S. presidents by the title "President."

The Bible gives many examples of people who are called to take a new path or profession and sometimes received new names. God called Abram to leave his country, his people, and his father's household to the land God would show him.[2] God also changed Abram's name to Abraham when God made a covenant with him to become "the father of many nations."[3] God called Moses from a burning bush to lead the Jews out of captivity in Egypt.[4] In the New Testament we learn about Jesus calling men to leave their professions to become his disciples. Before Jesus called them, Simon (later called Peter), Andrew, James, and John were fisherman,[5] and Matthew was a tax collector.[6]

Jesus's primary call to his disciples, and by inference to all people, is to "follow me." By following Jesus, Christians are called to a different life, a transcendent life focused on Jesus. The self-focused life becomes a God-focused life. It is a life surrendered to Jesus—a "higher calling" that results in a new perspective on life. A higher call engenders an eternal view with a focus on one's relationship with Christ and obedience to him, rather than a temporal view that is often disrupted by circumstances and marred by worry. Christians are called to love God and their neighbors. Jesus even gives his followers a special designation. He calls his disciples his "friends."[7]

The higher call to follow Jesus is a life-long journey with ups and downs, trials and triumphs. Followers of Christ have failures, as did much-admired characters in the Bible: Moses murdered an Egyptian forcing him into seclusion for 40 years before receiving his call to free the Jews; Peter denied Christ soon after promising that he would never do such a thing.

Although a higher call supersedes vocation, ministry, and even family as a focus, it informs choices Christians make in each of these areas. Every person whose story appears in this book understands their higher calling. They try to live by that calling daily. We have seen how God's call resulted in changing their attitudes, gave meaning to their lives, and, in some cases, resulted in career decisions at the prompting of God.

In this section, we further explore how God's call affects the lives and careers of Silicon Valley leaders.

Chapter 11
Following God's Call

Call is primarily about who we are and what we do all the time. Call isn't measured by outcomes – how much we achieve or accomplish – but through the process of following Jesus in and through it all.[1]
~ Mark Labberton

Neil Ahlsten and Kirk Perry are followers of Christ attuned to listen for His direction. Both men held enviable positions. Neil managed a team at Google responsible for driving new solutions to grow Google's revenue. Kirk led Procter & Gamble's (P&G) largest division—Global Family Care products—as its president. Both men, however, heard a call from God to change their career direction.

God called Neil to leave Google to start a company, and God called Kirk to leave P&G to come to Silicon Valley and to work at Google as its President of Brand Solutions.

Neil Ahlsten—When God Calls, You Better Show Up!

Why did Neil Ahlsten decide to leave a high-powered job at Google—what he refers to as "a very lucrative career in a very lucrative space?" He simply states, "When God calls, you better show up."

Neil began to heed God's call early in his life. As a sophomore at U.C. Berkeley, where he eventually graduated *summa cum laude* in mathematics, he was reading from Luke, Chapter 10. In that chapter, Jesus calls 70 of His disciples to go out with nothing—no money and no extra clothes—to share God's Word.[2] Neil says, "I felt—and this was very weird—God telling me to go do that." The following summer, Neil obeyed. He took a backpack and a Bible and hitchhiked from Berkeley to San Francisco to live on Haight Street for a week.

As he was reading his Bible on Haight Street, Neil came across a verse in 2 Thessalonians where the Apostle Paul says, "It is good to work."[3] Neil said to himself, "If someone comes to offer me a job, I will take it." Five minutes later, a man came by and offered Neil a job to clean his apartment. Neil found out that this man was prominent in the gay community as a writer. Neil took the job. After paying Neil $20, the man asked Neil if he needed a place to stay. Neil declined, saying he had a comfortable place in Golden Gate Park.

Two days later, Neil complained to God, "Why haven't you given me a place to stay?" Neil says that God responded to him saying, "I have. You didn't think I could use a gay Jewish man. I can use anybody." "That was a definitive point in my faith journey," says Neil. "It radically changed my life. I realized that God saw the world differently than I saw it, and in much more real and purposeful ways that I could ever imagine."

That period also helped Neil find the purpose of his life, which he says, "is to be in a posture of listening, to be obedient to what God is telling me to do, and to do what is right."

Several years later—in 2012—after Neil had earned a master's degree in Public Policy from Princeton, had gotten married and had children, and was working for Google, he sensed a new call from God. Neil was on a business trip in Africa when he felt God calling him to apply technology to Christian faith. He comments, "God put on my heart that the church, in general, was missing where technology was going and how it was being used."

Neil began to think about using mobile devices for prayer, but for the most part he says he thought it was "a dumb idea." That is, until early 2013, when God gave him a specific message. "While I was at church praying, I felt God pass over me in a humbling way. I was in tears when I heard Him say, 'You are not big enough to understand what I do in prayer.'" With that message, Neil began to look seriously at developing a prayer app.

A short time later, Neil received a confirmation when he was on a telephone call with Christian leader, Os Hillman. During the call, Hillman felt compelled to pass the phone to a colleague to pray for Neil. Neil recalls that although the man on the other end of the phone knew nothing about Neil and his ideas, the man began praying from John 15. Neil recalls:

> *"Abide in the vine" is what this guy kept saying. Abide, abide, abide – which is, of course, the name of our product. This guy said that he saw a network of people praying together and went through a list of things he was envisioning in great detail. He said all of this, yet he knew nothing about us. It was mind blowing.*

Neil's company is called Carpenter's Code. Carpenters has what business author, Jim Collins, would call a "Big, Hairy, Audacious Goal." Neil hopes to have 40 million people using the app called "Abide" to pray twice a week. Although this is a lofty goal, the company has made a good start. In 2014, the for-profit company raised $400K in seed money and launched Abide in February 2015. In just two months after the launch over 75,000 copies of the Abide app were downloaded in 180 countries, and over 1 million prayers were finished.

On the inside, Carpenter's Code looks like a typical Silicon Valley start-up with programmers working feverously in an open office, developing code and answering customer inquiries. But on the outside it is quite different. Although the company intends to make money for its shareholders and reward its employees, its mission is purely faith-based: "Creating tools to connect with God."

For his whole life as a follower of Jesus, Neil was in a posture ready to listen and obey God. Unlike Neil, Kirk Perry didn't fully surrender his life to Christ until he was an adult. It took a tragedy to get his full attention. Once attuned to God, however, Kirk was ready to obey.

Kirk Perry

Kirk grew up poor. "My family couldn't afford to buy me a real baseball glove when I was ten years old," says Kirk. His parents had three children by the time they were twenty-two years old and lived in a trailer for a period. Kirk was the oldest child. His parents survived on Welfare and Aid to Dependent Children for a year, which Kirk calls "both humbling and humiliating."

Poverty forced Kirk to work during school to pay for things beyond his basic needs and to save for college. He worked at various jobs, including as a waiter, truck driver, painter, and bartender. During one summer, he worked two jobs—driving a truck during the days and waiting tables in the evenings.

Through the help of people who came into his life, however, he was able to escape poverty as well as a low self-image that comes with being poor. "The theme of my story," says Kirk "is that people reached down and picked me up, even though there was a cost and no benefit to them whatsoever. They saw in me what I didn't see in myself."

A Little League coach encouraged Kirk and offered to buy him the baseball glove he needed if his parents couldn't afford one; a high school principal told Kirk he saw potential in him and put Kirk on his advisory board. His manager at a Wendy's restaurant—where Kirk worked between high school and college—saw potential in Kirk and wondered why he wasn't in college. The manager allowed Kirk to modify his work schedule so that he could attend school and work at the same time. Once in college, a professor who knew Kirk worked 60 hours a week and went to school full time, suggested he meet with an assistant dean to see if scholarship money happened to be available so that Kirk could attend college without having to work full time. Kirk remarks, "On the spot, the assistant dean agreed. He changed the trajectory of my life."

When Kirk graduated, he interviewed for finance and consulting positions at various companies. An undergraduate professor, however, talked to Kirk about Procter & Gamble (P&G), the premier marketing and general management company in the world. Kirk applied for and got a job in marketing. "I thought I'd be there three years and then go back to get my MBA." That didn't happen. Kirk loved the marketing and the holistic general manager training he received at P&G. He hoped that one day he would have the opportunity to work globally and as a general manager.

The opportunity came in 1997 when he was offered a position with P&G to work in South Korea. That was an eye-opening, life-changing experience for Kirk in many ways—both personally and professionally. "I was working in a different culture, and from a business standpoint it was a startup. It tested every one of my leadership, marketing, and business capabilities."

His time in Korea also marked a pivotal turning point in Kirk's faith. "For much of my life," Kirk comments, "I just mentally believed in God. From a heart standpoint, I didn't have a relationship with Him. When I was growing up, my family and I were 'Chr-easters—Christmas and Easter only Christians. We'd go to church when there were crises in our lives—like when my dad lost his job or when something difficult was happening. Then when things got better, we'd stop attending. It was always a very tactical, crisis-based relationship with God." After he had gotten married, Kirk and his wife attended church regularly "because we thought it was important for our kids." Kirk says that his wife, Jacki, was always a faithful follower of Christ. "She was so patient with me, but I didn't really have a relationship with Christ."

While in New York on a business trip in 1999 (he was living in South Korea at the time), he received a message from his wife who was home in Cincinnati with their children for the summer. His return call "took my breath away," says Kirk. His six-year-old daughter, Karly, was diagnosed with cancer.

On his trip home, Kirk called for an update on his daughter's condition from a pay phone at LaGuardia Airport. As his sister-in-law explained that Karly had kidney cancer and would need to have a kidney removed, Kirk started crying. To his surprise, an older woman standing behind Kirk had her hand on his shoulder the whole time and when he finished the call she gave him a bear hug. "She wiped the tears off and rubbed my cheek. We never exchanged a single word." Looking back, Kirk says, "I am pretty confident that God put an angel behind me while I was on that pay phone that day to make sure I knew that He was with me." To this day, he touches that phone bank every time he walks by it.

The next day, one of Karly's kidneys was removed. As Kirk was in the cancer ward of the hospital, he happened to walk by a room where he noticed a young girl "with something in her skull to drip chemo directly on her tumor." As he was staring at the girl for 15 to 30 seconds, he noticed the girl's dad out of the corner of his eye. Kirk apologized for staring. After a brief conversation, Kirk noticed the man's Bible. He asked the man, "How can you possibly believe that (pointing to the Bible), when that (pointing to his daughter) is going on?" The man replied that he would probably kill himself if he didn't believe and added, "It is the only thing that gives me hope. I know that my daughter is not going to be here very long, but every day is a gift, and God assures me of that in this book."

When Kirk got back to his room, he told the story to his wife and commented, "How do people think this way?" His wife replied, "That's exactly the way we should be thinking."

Karly's operation the next day was successful, but a month later a complication showed up. "Karly started writhing in great pain on the floor every 10 minutes," says Kirk. She was admitted to the hospital, and after a week of morphine buttons being pushed every 10 minutes and a nose tube draining everything from her stomach, the Perrys told the doctors, "We need to figure this out today, or we are moving her." The doctors ordered an MRI on Karly and concluded that she had a surgical adhesion that had resulted from removing the kidney and it was causing a colon blockage. The doctors also told Kirk they thought her colon was perforated and that they would "have to leave her open for two weeks to heal." This meant she would also have to have a colostomy bag. "I couldn't believe that my six-year-old daughter was not only going through chemo, but was going to have her gut open and was going to have a colostomy bag. What kind of a loving God lets that happen?"

Then something occurred that Kirk said he would never forget. As they rushed his daughter down to the operating room to prepare for surgery, Karly pulled the doctor down to her face and said, "Please help me, you have to stop the pain. I can't take it anymore." She then held Kirk's hand and said, "Daddy, please stop the pain. Please, Daddy, you can do it, please." Kirk and his wife wept as the doctors wheeled Karly to the operating room. They began waiting for what was supposed to be a four- or five-hour surgery when an hour into it the surgeon kicked open the door—still in surgical garments, mask, gloves, and all—to say, "Great news. We opened her up; there was no perforation. We clipped off part of the colon, sewed it back together, and she's in recovery."

Kirk and his wife fell to the ground weeping, knowing that Karly would be okay. When they got up, Jacki said something that completely changed Kirk's journey in following God. She said, "Can you imagine how God felt when Jesus was hanging on the cross and said, 'My God, my God, why have you forsaken me?' God could have stopped it. He had the power to do anything but chose not to. We would have given anything to stop Karly's pain, but we couldn't. That's how much He loves us!'"

For the first time, Kirk understood God's sacrificial love for everyone—Jesus died so that everyone could be saved. Kirk realized that God was with him all the time. "I had one of those transformational moments that you hear about sometimes. I used to not believe this, but at that moment for the first time, I understood that God was chasing me. God wanted a relationship with me. I dropped to my knees and thanked God for this tragedy. He was showing me a triumph and wanted to draw me nearer to Him."

Kirk Finds a New Calling

Going through the ordeal with his daughter and finding God changed Kirk's life. He fully surrendered his life to Him. In doing so, he became a better father, a better husband, and even a better employee. "Oddly," Kirk adds, "I was more on purpose at work." His career skyrocketed. He became one of the youngest general managers and presidents at Procter & Gamble. "I wasn't any better than anyone else. I was just incredibly focused on what was important and mattered and I was on fire for God."

Kirk found a new purpose. "I realized that God was calling me to be a workplace missionary, to be in a place where just by the way I acted, people noticed that I was different. I wanted people to look at me and ask, 'What's different about that guy? Why does he believe what he believes?' It created incredible conversations."

By 2013, Kirk was president of P&G's Global Family Care business that marketed well-known items such as Bounty, Charmin, and Puffs. P&G's CEO met with Kirk one day to give Kirk additional "retention" stock options because he was a key leader in the company's future and had further upside potential.

By all accounts, Kirk's life was flourishing. His family life was doing well; he was engaged in community activities, coached youth sports, and he was deeply involved in his church—Crossroads Church, a megachurch in Cincinnati. In fact, Crossroads asked Kirk to give sermons on occasion—quite a change from someone who had been, at best, a nominal Christian. And his career was on a fast track. He says he was "planted, growing, and content."

But Kirk sensed a new calling as well. "I suddenly started having this nagging feeling - 'Is this what God wants me to be?' 'Does he want me to be CEO of a company like Procter & Gamble?' I just had this feeling, but couldn't explain it."

Nominal Christian

The term "nominal Christian" often refers to someone who self-identifies as a Christian, and may even attend church regularly, but has not accepted Christ as his or her Savior, does not have a personal relationship with Christ, and does not recognize the need for personal repentance.

God Calls Kirk to Google and Silicon Valley

Kirk traveled to Silicon Valley with his management team to see if they could benefit from Silicon Valley practices. As part of the tour, his group met with one of Google's senior business leaders. In that meeting, the leader mentioned that Google had a position open for eighteen months and couldn't find the right person to fill it. "In a moment, I thought 'Whoa, she must be talking to me,' and I also thought quickly after that that I must be having delusions of grandeur!" says Kirk. However, the thought persisted for a week. "I kept having this feeling that I'm supposed to reach out to her and follow up."

His wife was not happy with the prospect: "Even if there is something there, there is no way I'm moving to California." But Kirk couldn't shake the feeling that God was calling him to something. He emailed the leader with whom he had met and asked if, in fact, she was talking directly to him about the position opening. She responded, "We heard you were perceptive … :)."

Kirk was elated but torn. He was interested in pursuing the position but didn't want to leave Cincinnati. "I was content with what I was doing. I was having a big impact on the city and was having a big impact in my faith community and my work."

As the prospect of an offer looked certain, Kirk decided to take a risk to see if this was God's urging or his ego driving him. He wanted to let the people at Google understand who he was as a person and particularly how important his faith was to him. He had recently delivered a sermon at Crossroads Church—a message in which he discussed his faith journey, including the impact of his daughter's illness and how he surrendered himself to God. He decided to send a link to the video of his message at Crossroads to his Google contact with the following thought, "This is who I am all the time. If this is a problem, then I'm probably not the right fit."

Kirk was surprised when the leader responded, "This is amazing. Google would love you. You would love Google. I hope we can make this work."

Kirk continued the interview process, but not without trepidation. He wondered why God was leading him in this new direction. Kirk talked with a close friend who was a mentor and spiritual advisor. He called his friend, who suggested that they pray together. His friend had recently parachuted for the first time and while praying envisioned Kirk floating to the earth in a parachute. His friend told Kirk, "God is asking you to step to the edge and take a leap for Him. He's got a plan for you." Kirk called Jacki and told her what had just happened. They agreed that God had ordained the move. Kirk accepted the offer and moved to Silicon Valley in December 2013.

Kirk's transition to Google and Silicon Valley was not easy. He was in a new position in a high-tech company, and was living in a new community with the need to find a church and make new friends. But he says, "I feel like God affirmed me every single step of the way." He says that he is still not sure why God has called him to Google and Silicon Valley but says that he is getting some clues.

Just after he accepted the offer, he heard from the leader who recruited Kirk. She told Kirk that he hadn't heard from her for several days because she was busy with her own child who was recently diagnosed with cancer. "I don't know why I am telling you this. I don't even know you very well, but for some reason I needed to share this with you because I know from the video you sent, that you and your wife have gone through a similar experience. And I don't know, but maybe you can help us get through this." Kirk says, "I felt like God took a big rubber stamp and just hit my passport to Google and said, 'Well done, good and faithful servant.'"

Kirk is getting other clues. By his willingness to share his journey of faith at events like the Silicon Valley Prayer Breakfast, which attracted over 700 people, Kirk has inspired many people of faith and those who are not yet believers.

Kirk was diagnosed with cancer in February 2015. Although cancer is a major issue for Kirk, he feels that the diagnosis is giving him other clues as to why he is in the Bay Area. Contrary to the advice of friends and colleagues, Kirk sent a video message to employees in his division that he had cancer. In that video, Kirk asked employees two things. First, he asked that they continue to drive the business in his absence. Second, he asked his group to pray for him—something almost never done so publicly by a leader in Silicon Valley. In return, Kirk says he received hundreds of affirming messages. Only God knows how many of those employees, seeing Kirk's faith, will consider faith themselves.

Finally, Kirk feels by having cancer while living in the Bay Area he is blessed to know that the Bay Area "is the home of some of the leading cancer specialists in the world." Kirk fully expects that his ordeal will simply result in a new chapter in his life and his testimony of faith.

Both Kirk Perry and Neil Ahlsten are men who have entrusted their lives to God. As a result, they were ready to hear God's call and respond. It was through prayer, friends, and even signs that they confirmed their calls. Most importantly, they obeyed. For both men—and for every follower of Christ—business and financial success is not guaranteed, even when one follows God's call. When asked about success, Neil replied, "God gave me no promise for success. My business is a ministry, and I am called to make an impact." God's ultimate call to followers of Christ is to follow Him, to be "good and faithful servants," and to be witnesses for Christ to others. Just as Jesus came to serve, He expects His followers to serve as well.

Chapter 12
Business as a Calling

Christians are gifted for and called to vocations of every type, including those vocations in the business world.[1]
~ Ken Eldred, founder of Silicon Valley companies Inmac and Ariba Technologies

Does business have meaning outside of making a living? For committed followers of Christ, business is much more than making a living. It is about making a difference and glorifying God. Let's look at the stories of two people, Deb Liu and Emily Liggett, to see how they view their careers.

Deb Liu, Facebook Executive

Deb Liu leads Facebook's Platform Product Group, which encompasses the developer and commerce products. This includes login, sharing, analytics for apps, games, payments, and app ads—functions critical to Facebook's commercial success. She is highly educated, having earned an MBA from Stanford and a BSE from Duke, and is perfectly suited for her role. She came to Facebook from PayPal where she was instrumental in building PayPal's eBay payments platform. At Facebook, Deb leads a group of 150 people based both in Silicon Valley and Seattle. Through her work, she has an impact on thousands of businesses and the lives of hundreds of millions of Facebook users.

Facebook exemplifies the newest breed of Silicon Valley companies. It attracts a young tech-savvy workforce bent on making their mark in the world. Unlike traditional Silicon Valley companies like Hewlett-Packard and Intel, sporting acres of cubicles and classical color schemes, Facebook workers thrive in an array of colors laboring side by side on workbenches in barn-like buildings with electrical and cable drops for their computers and large high-definition monitors.

Deb calls Facebook "an amazing place to work—one of those once-in-a-lifetime companies." She is excited by the company's overarching goal to make a major impact on the world by connecting people with friends, community, and information. Over one billion users can testify to its impact. Deb and her team are at the center of it all.

Business as a Way to Glorify God

Deb's Christian faith drew her to her role at Facebook. "Business is a calling and it is my calling. Not everyone is called to work as a pastor or in a church. We are called to wherever God places us, and can glorify Him in any job we have."

Many people look at work as drudgery, as something you do to make a living. Not Deb Liu. "God created work. From the moment He made Adam, He gave him a job: to name the animals, to care for them and His creation." She recalls an article by a Facebook research scientist who viewed his job as simply "getting people to click on ads." Although part of her job is related to ads, she views her job quite differently. "I want to see my job as a way to glorify God, not just a way to do something and have a vocation. I look at my job as a way to connect people, for people to have free expression, for people to write their life story so that they have a legacy for their children to see when they leave this earth."

Deb points out that God endows each person with certain talents and experiences that uniquely qualify them for specific jobs. Due to her tech and business experience, especially at PayPal, she feels particularly qualified for her work at Facebook. "God created us to have an impact. If I can't add value in my job and bring something unique to it, I shouldn't be in that role."

Deb loves working in business and specifically in high technology. "If you can just figure out the problem, it can have an impact on not a million people but a hundred million people." Her objective, however, goes beyond making an impact. She views her work as a form of worship. "God gave us the ability to do so much. He gave us gifts and talents. We can either bury them or multiply them. We glorify God when we multiply our talents."

The Parable of the Talents

Parables are stories that Jesus tells to illustrate a point. In the so-called "Parable of the Talents,"[2] Jesus commends the servants who invested their talents and brought the owner a multiple return on his investment, and condemns the one who didn't. A key point that Jesus makes is that His followers are to invest their time, talents, and resources, (which all originate from God) to bless others and to further His kingdom. His followers will be held accountable to God for how they used the resources they are given.

Deb invests her talents to produce results, but also hopes to provide a good example to her fellow workers. She recoils at the statement Mahatma Gandhi once said, "I like your Christ, I do not like your Christians. Your Christians are so unlike Christ."[3]

Deb makes it a point to let people know that she is a Christian. She wears a cross daily and is open about her faith on her personal Facebook page—which she knows her fellow workers read. "Perhaps 1% of my colleagues ask me about my faith, but the other 99% can witness it."

Specifically, she strives to treat everyone well. "I want each person who sees me to believe they are the only person I care about for the time I am with them. I believe that is what God does for us." She works hard to help make each individual and each team successful.

Deb points specifically to Philippians 4:6-7 in the Bible as a source of peace. "Do not be anxious about anything, but in every situation, by prayer and petition, with thanksgiving, present your requests to God. And the peace of God, which transcends all understanding, will guard your hearts and your minds in Christ Jesus."

Part of Deb's witness to others is the peace she shows in times of stress. "The peace of God transcends everything," she says. "It is incumbent on us as Christians to seek out that peace that transcends understanding. If you aren't the type of person people like or want to work with, would they want to embrace your faith?"

Struggles with Faith

Although Deb is a longtime follower of Christ, growing up with Christian parents and attending church her whole life, she sometimes struggles with her faith. She admits to having a hard time reconciling all the suffering in the world with a loving God who allows it. She doesn't understand, for example, how God allowed her father, a committed believer, to suffer and die from cancer at a fairly young age. She also struggles with living in the Silicon Valley culture where so many bright people are not Christian; many are indifferent to Christian faith and some vehemently oppose it.

In the end, she relies on the promises of God and His love. "I cannot accept the alternative that life is meaningless and devoid of purpose." She trusts that God has a bigger plan that she cannot comprehend. Her experience growing up as one of the few Asians in South Carolina may also help her deal with the counter-cultural experience and isolation Christians sometimes feel in Silicon Valley.

As the mother of three young children, Deb is concerned with the need to balance family and work, as are many Silicon Valley workers. She recognizes the challenge that a demanding tech job brings to her faith. "The enemy of faith is not the lack of faith, but the lack of time." The busyness of life can get in the way of developing a relationship with Christ and deepening faith. "But God has given us an amazing capacity to do things," she says. "It is simply a matter of focus. My calling is not just work, but life."

When her children were very young, she did not travel. As her children have gotten older, she limits the time she travels. Her husband, an attorney, offers much help when Deb's job does require additional time.

She makes faith a priority by finding time to engage in a weekly Bible study and by consistent church attendance with her husband and children.

Business is a calling for Deb Liu. It is an expression of her faith. It is a place where she can apply her God-given talents for good and be a faithful Christian witness for others to see. For Deb Liu, work is not her god, but a way to glorify God. Like Deb, Emily Liggett is a bright, talented woman who is called to the workplace, and is having an impact.

Emily Liggett—CEO of NovaTorque

It is unusual to find a female CEO of a manufacturing company anywhere, but especially in Silicon Valley—an area with few manufacturing companies and few female CEOs. But Emily Liggett is the leader of NovaTorque, a manufacturer of energy-efficient electric motors. She is an effective leader, an accomplished engineer, and a humble, committed follower of Christ.

Business Background

Emily graduated from Purdue University with a BS in chemical engineering and joined DuPont as a process engineer. Purdue recognized Emily for her accomplishments by granting her the Outstanding Chemical Engineer Award in 1999 and the Distinguished Engineering Award in 2004.

With a desire to sharpen her business skills, she attended Stanford's Graduate School of Business, where she earned an MBA in 1984. Her career includes senior positions at large publicly held companies—Raychem, Tyco—and CEO of Capstone Turbine, Elo TouchSystems, and startup Apexon (now Symphony Software).

She started at NovaTorque in 2009 after the company raised its Series A financing. NovaTorque is a new electric motor company in an industry that is well over 100 years old. What distinguishes NovaTorque, Emily says, is the company's innovation. "We offer a significant leap forward in electric motor cost effectiveness and energy efficiency."

Faith Background

Emily grew up on a farm in Indiana in a Christian family with believing parents and grandparents. In the town of approximately 200, Christianity was simply part of the culture. Emily reflects: "If you went to town, the question wasn't, 'Do you go to church?' The question was 'Which church do you go to?' You were either Catholic or Protestant."

It was in college that Emily came face to face with people from other faith traditions and with people who didn't believe at all. A summer job at Bell Labs in New Jersey drove the point home. "I had a boss who explained to me that something was wrong if you didn't divorce and get remarried because it meant that you essentially hadn't grown and developed. I had this awakening that there were other people with completely different ideas." Coming to the Bay Area for graduate school and working in the area was eye-opening as well. She realized that she was in the minority as a Christian.

Over time, Emily's faith deepened. Bible studies, scripture reading, and discussions with mentors, including her husband, helped her. "My husband is an Indiana farm boy with a strong faith background. As we moved around the world, we could be our own little small group, with Bible studies and prayer time."

As a trained scientist, Liggett confronted the alleged conflict between faith and reason. She looked at the evidence for faith. "I had to think it through," she says. "And I looked at people who are a lot wiser than I am. C.S. Lewis dealt with that head on. He took a logical, reasoned approach to faith. That was instructive. For me, faith and reason coexist."

For Emily, her faith is not only intellectual but emotional as well. "I feel the presence of God all the time. I see His handiwork everywhere, especially when I am quiet—out of doors in nature—when I am with a newborn baby, and in both joyous and sorrowful times. I feel myself calm down. My heart doesn't race. I just sense that I am in the presence of God. I don't question His existence, although I don't understand some of the things that happen and don't know if I will ever fully understand."

Faith at Work

Emily lives out her faith every day at work with the guidance of biblical principles. It starts with integrity. She quotes Jesus in Matthew 5:37: "Let your yes be yes, and your no be no." She also strives to treat people fairly. "I am careful not to have a bias in hiring and promoting people—whether it is age, gender, marital status, or anything else. And I am careful not to impose my faith on anyone."

Transparency is an offshoot of integrity. "I just try being open and honest with people." She goes on to stress the importance of being direct. "Matthew made it clear; if you have an issue with someone, you go one-on-one and talk."[4]

Humility is at the core of who she is. "When I grew up, it was a big deal to my grandparents and parents that we kids 'not have a big head.' That was actually the term they used. If you brought home a report card and there was an A minus, and everything else was As, it was the A minus they would discuss. It wasn't a negative thing. It was simply, 'You are not perfect. There is room for improvement.' It was their way to keep us humble."

Balance

Like Deb, Emily confides that her biggest personal challenge, especially when her children were at home, was maintaining a balance between work and family. For Emily, balance was a special challenge with a working husband and four children. She offers an interesting perspective. "Every day is its own day. You can't achieve perfect balance every day. You try to get balance over a week, or over a month. There will be times when things are crazy at work, and you need to spend extra time. There will be other times when the family time is important, so you take time off from the office, and other people will have to cover work for you."

It helped that her husband had a reasonably flexible schedule. "It was a 100% team effort. When my husband, Dave, was doing international work, I would take a job with no travel. Or if I were traveling a lot, he would make sure he didn't travel. And we have this extended network—our church small group—to call. Our kids were and are loved by many different people."

But achieving balance and giving children the attention they deserve is hard. "You're always moving between the two (work and family)." She describes two principles that were helpful. "We tried not to work on Sunday. That was family day. There might be a rare exception, but it was a big deal. If we did, then Saturday became our Sabbath."

Second, she and her husband shared taking their children to and from school. One of us would go to work early and come home early. The other would go late and come home late."

Life Purpose and Principles

One of Emily's guiding principles comes from Philippians 4:13, a verse other Silicon Valley leaders point to. The verse reads: "I can do all this through him who gives me strength."

"When things seemed impossible," Emily says, "whether personal, family, or at work, good things happened. When I wanted more time with my kids, I had the opportunity to job share with a woman who was going to seminary. That was a fabulous relationship." After having her fourth child, she left work. But shortly after leaving, her husband's company was acquired. He became a stay-at-home dad, and Emily re-entered the workforce.

Emily describes her purpose this way: "I want to glorify God in whatever I do—whether as a stay-at-home mom, starting a company, taking over a company for someone else, being on the board of directors, or working on staff for a year at Menlo Presbyterian Church. Each time I felt that was where I should be for that season."

Leading NovaTorque is where Emily Liggett's calling is today. Although it is unusual to find a woman in Silicon Valley running a manufacturing company, she doesn't look at it that way. "I haven't thought about it very much. I like products. I like things I can touch. And I have been well trained for what I am doing." She is a remarkable but humble person who is living out her God-given purpose.

For Deb Liu and Emily Liggett, following Christ is their primary calling. In addition, business is their vocational calling. God provides each person with unique skills and experience and calls people to different purposes and professions. Calling is clear when it is to the clergy or non-profit work helping the poor and disadvantaged. Calling, however, is broader than that. Theologian Frederick Buechner once wrote, "The place God calls you is the place where your deepest gladness and the world's deep hunger meet."[5]

God calls people not only to vocational ministry and nonprofit work but to business and other professions as well. In business, followers of Christ have the opportunity to demonstrate their faith by the way they work—by the decisions they make, by how they treat customers, vendors, and fellow employees, and by working to the best of their ability. Behaving in such a way is what Christian business people mean when they use the phrase "glorifying God." They want help their organizations and the people in their companies to succeed. They want to be positive examples that reflect Jesus' character.

> Christian business people want to be positive examples that reflect Jesus' character.

Chapter 13
Called as an Entrepreneur

The entrepreneur always searches for change, responds to it, and exploits it as an opportunity.[1]
~ Peter Drucker

The startup mentality pervades Silicon Valley, the entrepreneurial and venture capital center of the world. Not evident from the outside, however, are the entrepreneurs who feel called to start businesses that honor and glorify God—some with explicitly faith-based products, most like other Silicon Valley startups, with technology products aimed at solving problems or making life better.

Andrew Laffoon—Called to be an Entrepreneur

Andrew Laffoon is living out his calling as an entrepreneur. He is co-founder and CEO of Mixbook, a company aimed at making photo books and photo sharing more convenient.

Growing up in a small town in eastern North Carolina, Andrew found that he liked building things—Legos, model airplanes, and electronic equipment, especially computers. He sensed a "calling" from God at age 14 when he heard a talk by a Christian entrepreneur who had a knack for building successful businesses. The entrepreneur started businesses to create wealth that he could give away to help the disadvantaged, and to spread the Word of God. As a follower of Christ at a young age, Andrew saw the possibility to meld his faith with his interest in building things. Business provided the perfect opportunity to do so.

Andrew moved with his parents to the Los Angeles area when he was in high school. With an interest in programming and the Internet and a desire to run a business, Andrew started his first venture—a web design and development agency. The consulting work was successful enough that Andrew continued with it when he entered the University of California, Berkeley in 2001.

At Berkeley, Andrew met a like-minded entrepreneur in his classmate, Aryk Grosz. The two partnered to enter an entrepreneurship competition. Not only did they win the competition, they realized that they made a great team.

Founded Mixbook

Andrew and Aryk often brainstormed startup ideas with their entrepreneurship professor, Jon Burgstone. The professor rejected all their business concepts until one day Aryk and Andrew suggested an idea to build an online service to create school yearbooks. They were excited that their professor thought this was such a good idea. Having grown up homeschooled, Andrew had little experience with yearbooks. But with a shot of confidence from their professor, Andrew and Aryk decided to start a business based on the yearbook idea. Their company, Mixbook, was born in 2006.

The founders needed to raise money. They met with 50 venture firms. All rejected the idea. "No one wanted to back a couple of young kids with a vision but no product," says Andrew. The yearbook idea also wasn't getting traction with possible customers. They did find one yearbook teacher, however, who loved the idea; that is, until the founders demonstrated the software to the teacher. "His jaw dropped when he realized that our product would destroy traditional yearbooks. He refused to allow it at his high school."

That evening, however, Andrew and Aryk met with a friend, Joshua Chodniewicz, a fellow Christian and a founder of Art.com. Joshua suggested that Aryk and Andrew pivot from yearbooks to the broader photo book market. The suggestion resonated with Andrew. He enjoyed putting together photo books. "I had already created two photo books, but the existing photo sites were clumsy to use and not integrated into social sites where people were putting their photos," says Andrew. Within 24 hours, Josh and Mike Marston, also a founder of Art.com, offered to provide initial funding for Mixbook.

In true entrepreneurial style, the Mixbook founders imagined a way to transform the way photo books were put together. They envisioned a flexible, easy-to-use website that would allow people to collaborate in building photo books. They launched the company's first product in early 2007.

Initially, the product struggled in the marketplace. Not deterred, a few months later they introduced their first application on Facebook called "Photobooks." People loved the product. Soon Mixbook had millions of users. With product acceptance, Mixbook was able to raise $800K in funding from Labrador Ventures and the Band of Angels. Within a year, the company turned profitable and started growing rapidly. In 2011, the company raised an additional $10 million in venture funding.

The company caught the attention of business publications. In December 2012, *Inc. Magazine* recognized Andrew and Aryk in its annual "Top 30 under 30"—a list of entrepreneurs to watch. In 2013, *Forbes Magazine* named Andrew one of "America's Most Promising CEOs under 35."

Andrew's Faith Journey

Andrew's story, however, is not just about entrepreneurial success. His Christian faith shapes his vision and passion. "I am called to be an entrepreneur and to be in high-tech. I want to use my platform to make an impact for God and an impact for the world in a meaningful way."

Andrew says that the story of Daniel in the Bible inspires him. Daniel is a biblical character who lived 500 to 600 hundred years before Christ. Daniel was a person of Jewish ancestry and faith who exerted great influence in the non-Jewish Babylonian and Persian empires. In a similar fashion, Andrew hoped that business would provide a platform for him to honor and glorify Christ in a secular world.

His faith journey, like that of nearly all Christians, is not a straight line. It has twists, turns, and challenges. As a home-schooled child growing up in a Christian home in the Bible-belt, he didn't waiver in his faith. At Berkeley, however, he met people with widely different philosophies and beliefs. Different beliefs were not entirely new to Andrew. His dad, who taught a philosophy class, had exposed Andrew to philosophers like Hegel, Kant, and Descartes, who had different, non-Christian, approaches to God. In addition, Andrew took philosophy courses at Berkeley.

As he was confronted by passionate and intelligent non-Christian students and professors, Andrew realized that he had to make a choice. "Berkeley is a place that does not accept non-answers very well. As a Christian at Berkeley, you have to be really serious about your faith or stop believing. Being halfway doesn't work. Ultimately, you have to choose what you think is right and what to believe." Andrew not only weighed the evidence for Christian faith, but fell back on his experience with faith and his relationship with Christ, which he knew was real. He chose to believe and to live it out every day.

Living Out His Calling in Business

Andrew believes that God not only provides a calling, but also provides the ability to fulfill the calling, and with its fulfillment comes passion. His passion is readily evident in how he describes Mixbook. "We are a company of fanatics. We are driven to make the entire photo book experience exceptional because anything less would be unthinkable. We are passionate about building something truly great, no matter the effort."

Every start-up company faces challenges that threaten its existence. Mixbook is no exception. In the company's early years, Andrew and Aryk went through years with little and often no pay. They faced repeated rejections from investors, potential customers, and job candidates. In 2008, the company nearly ran out of money. "It was at that point that I was feeling terrible," says Andrew. "I would come home, eat dinner, and throw-up, I was so nervous."

His Christian faith, however, helped him get through the early struggles. "I prayed. When my mental and emotional resources were depleted, I had access to a deeper spiritual place that I could go to restore my energy and hope—an internal place of peace that couldn't be shaken by circumstances. It wasn't just about having rose-colored lenses or expecting a divine miracle, although I've experienced that, too. It was that I could stand on a rock, a firm foundation. I could stand confidently in the hope of God's promises and know that what I see is not all that there is. If it were not for my faith and trust in God, I don't know what I would have done."

In running the business, Andrew relies on two important biblical principles—integrity and respect. "Aryk and I decided early on that integrity and honesty were essential in running the business. We committed to doing what we say we are going to do. We are not going to lie, and we are not going to mislead others." Also, treating people with respect, dignity, and love is part of the Mixbook culture. But Andrew is quick to observe, "Love also means being brutally honest. Jesus was, after all, brutally honest with the Pharisees."[2]

Called to Family

Faith helps Andrew navigate the demands of running an entrepreneurial business with his role as a husband and father of two young children. "As much as my calling is to be in business, it is also my calling to be a good husband and dad. My calling is to love my wife and kids more than I love myself. My calling is to put their needs in front of my own, as much as it is to put the needs of my employees ahead of mine."

There is a significant tension for any entrepreneur between the amount of time required to lead a start-up company and the need and desire to spend time with family. Andrew admits that balancing these demands is a challenge, but has found a way to ease the tension. He established the habit to come home to have dinner with his family. "I highly value dinner time with my family. I'm typically back online at ten in the evening, however. I also commit to at least one full day at home with family on weekends."

Faith is the key ingredient that helps Andrew navigate the challenges inherent in leading an entrepreneurial business and caring for a family. Andrew also understands that practicing spiritual disciplines like worship and prayer, and having the fellowship of godly people are important to keeping a focus on God and staying accountable. Among other spiritual activities, Andrew hosts a weekly prayer meeting at his office. Around seven to twelve men participate, depending on travel and other commitments. Most of the participants are under 40 years old and work in high-tech jobs. They pray for each other, hold each other accountable, and help keep each other grounded in their faith.

Andrew answered God's call on his life. So did Victor Ho, co-founder of FiveStars, a company offering a universal customer loyalty card and services.

Victor Ho—Called to Start a Company in Silicon Valley

Victor answered God's call to leave a promising career in consulting and move from New York to Silicon Valley. He and colleague, Matt Doka, had a vision on how to improve customer loyalty for local merchants. Local merchants are at a disadvantage competing against large retailers that employ retailer-specific loyalty cards by which customers can achieve rewards and discounts. While engaged in their careers, Victor and Matt harbored a dream to provide a universal loyalty card. They saw the opportunity to provide a sophisticated but easy-to-use technology to allow local merchants to get to know and communicate directly with their customers.

The seeds for starting a company were planted when Victor worked as an intern at Goldman Sachs. He had a roommate who incessantly talked about startups. The idea intrigued Victor. Later, at the large management consulting firm, McKinsey & Company, in New York, he helped Fortune 500 companies manage their customer loyalty and retention programs. He met Matt while working at McKinsey. Matt was also a Christian. The two became good friends and soon began discussing the idea for starting a company around the idea of a universal loyalty card and service.

As Victor considered starting the business, he faced a critical decision. He was interviewing for jobs in California with two big private equity firms. A position at a private equity firm would have brought Victor an important addition to his resume and considerable money. But God intervened as he was at the San Francisco airport on his way home following the final rounds of interviews with the private equity firms. The flight was delayed. "As I was waiting, I felt God telling me very clearly, 'Victor, you know what you are supposed to do. Why are you such a huge coward about it?'" Victor called the firms where he was interviewing and withdrew his applications. He contacted Matt, and both decided to go forward with the plans for the business.

FiveStars

The transition was not easy. Both gave up lucrative careers and needed to learn computer programming. During the summer and fall of 2010, they worked feverously putting together a business plan and teaching themselves to program. "We were living on almost nothing," says Victor.

"I think that over the years God was trying to crush me from having any desire for money. He tells me just to let go."

Victor learned a lesson about letting go of money early in his career when he first moved to New York. He didn't worry much about money for most of his life. His family didn't have much. They lived in a low-cost area, and were frugal. But New York was a different story. Victor had taken a substantial pay cut to join McKinsey. He struggled to get by financially. But one day, he found that he had accumulated some money in his checking account. Just when he started feeling secure, he heard a message from God to "give it all away." He questioned God but obeyed. To his amazement, he continued to get by and even started saving money. From that point forward, he trusted God's provision, didn't worry about money, and continued to be generous. That lesson served him well as an entrepreneur.

> Victor trusted God and obeyed. Trust and obedience go hand-in-hand for the follower of Christ.

To receive advice and resources for their startup, Victor and Matt joined Y Combinator, a prestigious incubator located in San Francisco, where startup companies get space and advice from advisors. Upon joining, they received a stipend of $20,000. In late December 2010, however, as the money was running out, they received an invitation to an evening meeting with other entrepreneurs in residence. Much to their surprise, it was announced at the meeting that some investors, who had just made considerable money from investments in other companies, were offering $150,000 in what Ho called "basically free money" to each company associated with Y-Combinator at the time.

What was remarkable to Victor was that just two weeks before receiving the $150K, he was debating whether to make a significant annual donation to a mission organization he supported. But, of course, he had no income. This would be the first time he donated while earning no income. He would have to pull money out of the savings that he was living on. Having learned a lesson in New York about being obedient and and not tied to his money, he made the donation. Victor views the $150K FiveStars received as another lesson from God to trust His providence.

The funding allowed FiveStars to hire people, complete product development, and launch the product. Over the next several months, FiveStars raised additional venture funding that allowed the firm to hire staff and market the product. The company took off.

By June 2015, FiveStars had grown to 250 employees and had attracted thousands of merchants and in excess of a million cardholders. Such rapid growth is a rarity, even in venture financed businesses. The company is located in downtown San Francisco in a funky, multistory building with a brick interior. Like tech startups of the day, it has an open office layout with employees working on benches with electrical and cable drops powering PCs and large monitors. Snacks and games are easily available for employees needing a break.

Victor acknowledges that hard work, great employees, and investment capital contributed to the company's early success, but credits God with helping it all come together. "God has been directing my path very clearly along the way to bring me and the company to where we are today." He runs his business based on biblical principles. "Biblical principles are also good business principles," says Victor. He points to the principles of love and compassion, and the importance of relationships as essential to the way FiveStars operates.

He has a large goal for FiveStars. "We want to help redeem the transactional nature of commerce and believe society will be better off if we do. People will go through the day happier and be more generous. Our end goal is to make the world more relational." Having a large vision, which Victor says came from God, has helped the company get through the tough times all startups experience—investor and customer rejections, and the lack of money.

As CEO, Victor drives the culture. He strives to build a family-like atmosphere and has made philanthropy a cornerstone of that culture. Every quarter, the company allows employees to take a half-day off to serve at local charities. Prayer is also important to Victor. When the company first started, he would pray for the company at company town hall meetings. As the company got larger, however, he stopped praying publically so as not to offend employees not comfortable with Christian prayer. He does pray privately for the company and its employees. In addition, the company now offers an optional weekly prayer group and Bible Study. "Ultimately, I want to create a work environment where everyone is accepted and can bring their whole selves to work, including their personal beliefs. We work hard at having no discrimination. I don't think Jesus would be happy if we favored some people just because they were believers."

As with all new companies, the risk of failure is large. Victor offers a unique perspective. "Even if the company goes down in flames, I want to make sure we will be 'lights of the world.'" In that statement, Victor is referring to Jesus's proclamation to his disciples as recorded in Matthew 5: 14-16 "to be lights of the world." —to let people see their faith and good deeds so that God will be glorified, and others will be drawn to faith.[3]

Both Victor Ho and Andrew Laffoon are fulfilling God's purposes for their lives and their call as entrepreneurs. While financial success is important in keeping their businesses going, more importantly they are leading lives of character, endeavoring to obey and honor God in all their actions.

Chapter 14
Called to Serve

Everybody Can Be Great,
Because Everybody Can Serve.[1]
~ Dr. Martin Luther King

Years ago I heard a talk by sociologist, pastor, and author, Dr. Tony Campolo. Although I don't always agree with what Dr. Campolo has to say, I found a question he asked the audience thought-provoking. He asked, "What do you want your children to be when they grow up?" The word "happy" immediately came to my mind. According to a study, Campolo said that most American mothers would answer "happy," as I did. In Japan, he said, most mothers answered "successful." After World War II, success became the goal for children of many Japanese families.

In the family in which he grew up, Campolo believes that his Italian immigrant parents would have answered "good." To be "good," we sometimes have to sacrifice happiness and success.

"Good" was how Jesus lived his life. He served other people and implores his followers to do the same. Service is a basic tenet of Christian faith. Servant-leadership is a common way Christian leaders in Silicon Valley describe their management style. They seek to serve God, customers, and employees. And service is a lifestyle that doesn't stop at work; it extends to family, church, and the community.

Each person in this book viewed their work as a way to serve and fulfill their purpose; at the same time they were grateful for their material success knowing it was a blessing from God. In turn, they were generous with their resources. Let's look at three Silicon Valley business leaders who are called to serve.

> **Mark 10:43-45**
> "...For even the Son of Man did not come to be served, but to serve, and to give his life as a ransom for many."

Ken Yeung

Ken Yeung is a quiet, friendly, humble man with an infectious smile and always a good word to say. Like other Silicon Valley entrepreneurs, he is hardworking, driven, and has a vision for the future. His company, Prince of Peace Enterprises (POP), shares similarities with other successful Silicon Valley companies—a clear breakthrough that propelled the company to the next level. But Ken's story is not about high technology, venture capital funding, or a public offering.

Ken was born in China during the Communist Revolution. His father was jailed as a suspected capitalist because he was the son of a successful farmer. With no means to support her eight children, Ken's mother had to give away two of her daughters. Also, she had her oldest son take Ken, her younger son, to live with the boys' grandfather in Hong Kong.

Although Ken and his family were not Christian, he attended a government-subsidized Christian school in Hong Kong. Life changed for Ken at that school when he came under the influence of a teacher from England, who was a Christian missionary. "She really cared about us," remembers Ken. "She often invited the students to the park for picnics and afternoon tea as a way to get to know us better. She taught us scripture, and we often prayed together. I realized that I wanted to be just like her."

Following his teacher's example, Ken committed his life to Christ. He was grateful for the help he received from her and others who helped him during the difficult period of separation from his parents. Ken recalls saying a prayer at the time that became his life mission: "God, prepare me so that I can help people when I have a chance." For starters, he decided to attend Bible school.

In 1974, he earned a Master's degree in social work and international social policy from the University of Hawaii. Ken intended to return to Hong Kong to work for the government in the area of East-West relations. His career direction changed, however, when Ken's father was released from jail and moved to San Francisco. Ken joined his father in 1975 and started working as a ministerial assistant at a Chinese church helping Vietnamese refugees, while he sought to continue to fulfill his promise to God to help people. Through his work, he helped over 100 refugee families establish themselves in the U.S.

Unbeknown to Ken at the time, his work with the Vietnam refugees caught the attention of a Chinese government official who later, as we will see, helped Ken pursue another dream.

Called to Business as a Ministry

Working as an assistant pastor, Ken realized after several years that pastoring was no longer his calling. He had good business and administrative skills and felt that business could be his ministry for helping people.

He made a promise to God. "Regardless of what I do, whether in business or anything, I want to be a genuine Christian. If You are leading me to business, I want to acknowledge and remind myself that I am Your servant and Your steward and want to manage the business for You."

In 1983, Ken founded his business and named it "Prince of Peace," a title used for Jesus. Ken chose the name to remind him of his promise to God to honor him and to help others. He started Prince of Peace Enterprises (POP) to sell health-related products, most notable of which was Tiger Balm, a soothing cream manufactured in Singapore with over a 100-year history of healing people in Asia.

For the first few years, nearly all the company's customers were in the Chinese community. But at a trade show for sports trainers in Texas things changed. A San Francisco 49er trainer, Lindsey McLean, came by the booth and told Yeung how much he liked Tiger Balm. Ken was surprised because Lindsey was not Chinese. Lindsey told

Ken that he had purchased Tiger Balm in Chinatown. Boldly, Ken asked Lindsey if he thought the 49ers would endorse the product. "No," Lindsey said, "the team does not endorse products, but individuals can." Ken asked Lindsey if he would endorse the product, but Lindsey declined. When Ken returned to the Bay Area, he sent more samples to Lindsey and approached him again, this time asking if he thought Joe Montana would endorse Tiger Balm. Lindsey agreed to introduce Ken to Joe Montana's agent. Looking back, Ken sees Lindsey's willingness to help as part of God's plan for his business.

A Breakthrough for the Business

Montana's agent told Ken that Montana had just signed an endorsement deal with Pepsi ® and his minimum endorsement fee was $1 million. As a developing business with minimal cash flow, $1 million was way out of range for Prince of Peace. But Ken persisted. He continued to send samples to the 49er trainer and Montana.

Then, Montana injured his back. Fortunately for Montana and for Ken, Montana's back was treated with Tiger Balm and Montana's sore back greatly improved. Montana became a big fan of Tiger Balm and agreed to endorse the product for only $50,000. With Montana's radio commercials in the Bay Area, Tiger Balm's sales grew dramatically. With the 49ers continued success and Super Bowl wins, Tiger Balm went national, and sales skyrocketed.

Sales of Tiger Balm, which is available at major retailers like Wal-Mart® and Walgreens®, account for approximately one-third of Prince of Peace's revenue. American ginseng tea represents another one-third, and other specialty products account for the remainder.

Measuring Success

Ken's primary measure of success is not the company's revenue, profits, or number of employees. Success to Ken is to continue to serve and honor God in running his business and in serving his employees and people in need. He provides a positive, professional, and family-like culture at POP and delivers quality products to his customers. Also, Ken fulfills his God-given desire to serve others by supporting a variety of charitable organizations, both personally and through his company.

Ken personally supports local charities like the Teo Chew Community Center in Chinatown for seniors where he served as the organization's president for several years. He has helped a Christian missionary coordinate the adoption of over 100 orphans from China. Ken and his wife adopted a girl. Ken also started the Christian Entrepreneurs Association (formerly called the Chinese Entrepreneurs Association) in Silicon Valley. The association features events and activities around the topics of entrepreneurship and faith in business.

Prince of Peace Foundation

God had an even bigger plan for Ken. He put on Ken's heart the desire to go back to his roots in China where he had left as a child, to help special-needs children who are often neglected and not adopted. To help meet the need, Ken started the Prince of Peace Foundation with profits from Prince of Peace Enterprises. The Foundation funded an orphanage, Prince of Peace Children's Home (POPCH), on the outskirts of Beijing. The home opened in 2003.

It was no easy task to navigate the Chinese bureaucracy to start the orphanage. The government official who was impressed with Ken's heart for helping Vietnamese refugees years earlier helped Ken to get around the red tape and biases against U.S. involvement in China. He also helped Ken secure World Vision, a well-respected international charity, as the organization to manage the orphanage.

In the summer of 2015, Ken put together a conference in Beijing called "Beyond Dreams" to create awareness of the needs of orphaned and special-needs children in China and to raise money to support agencies caring for them. The conference was sponsored by the Prince of Peace Foundation and featured talks by well-known Christian celebrities like professional basketball player, Jeremy Lin, and singers and entertainers from Taiwan and Hong Kong. The event drew 6,000 people at one of the former Olympics sites and was viewed by over 100 million people online.

In addition to POPCH, the Prince of Peace Foundation helps victims of floods and earthquakes in China, supports educational organizations, and contributes tens of thousands of dollars each year to the local community.

Ken is grateful to God for directing his life and giving him his calling as a servant to accomplish so much. Philippians 4:13 in the Bible is particularly meaningful to him. The verse reads, "I can do everything through Him who gives me strength."

Tom Gutshall is another humble Silicon Valley executive who, like Ken, is called to serve through both his business and charitable work.

Tom Gutshall

Tom's passion is to make a difference in people's lives. He has had a distinguished background leading health-related companies, such as Cepheid, a publicly-held diagnostics company he co-founded. At the same time, he supports several charities, including CityTeam, a nonprofit organization helping the poor and disadvantaged. At CityTeam, he is active as the organization's longtime chairman. Faith is what drives his passion and his calling.

Tom earned his BS degree in chemical engineering from the University of Delaware and did post-graduate work in industrial management at the West Virginia University and the University of Missouri. He also completed the Marketing Management Program at the Harvard Business School. For 20 years, he progressed rapidly in executive positions at the leading bulk pharmaceutical companies Union Carbide and Mallinckrodt.

Tom came to Silicon Valley in 1981, as a vice president of Syntex Corporation in Palo Alto. In 1989, he was appointed executive vice president and helped Syntex become one of the 25 largest pharmaceutical companies in the world. He left Syntex after its acquisition by Roche in 1994 to take a position as president and COO of CV Therapeutics in Palo Alto, a biopharmaceutical company focused on cardio-vascular medicine. He left that operating role in 1996 while retaining a board position to co-found Cepheid.

Cepheid is an innovative microdiagnostics company with an emphasis on DNA testing. Cepheid was mentioned in David Persing's story in Chapter 9 for its breakthrough products helping to stop the spread of tuberculosis and Ebola, among other infectious diseases. Tom worked as the company's CEO from 1996 through 2002 as its chairman from 1996 through 2013, and currently serves as a director on Cepheid's board.

Cepheid is a Silicon Valley success story. Founded in 1996, the company was funded by angel investors and venture capitalists and went public in June 2000. The company raised $36 million in its public offering. By June 2015, the company reached a market value well over $4 billion.

Cepheid received national attention after the anthrax scare following the events of 9/11. The company worked at a feverish pace with a business partner to produce testing systems for the U.S. Postal service to detect traces of anthrax in the mail in their efforts to protect the public.

Philanthropy

Tom's business success tells only part of the story of the impact he has had on others. With a passion to make a difference, philanthropy and active participation in nonprofit organizations are of great interest to him.

He joined the board of CityTeam in 1982 and became the organization's chairman in 1986. During that time, CityTeam grew from an urban storefront ministry helping the homeless in San Jose to an organization providing services and residential facilities to the homeless and those addicted to drugs and alcohol. It also started providing services to abused women and their children.

In addition, CityTeam now engages in spiritual outreach efforts in the Bay Area and across the globe. The results are eye-opening. Since CityTeam began its evangelistic effort called "Disciple Making Movements" in 2004, it has helped form more than 28,000 churches worldwide with nearly 1 million new disciples in those churches. CityTeam's focus for its Disciple Making Movements is in Muslim-dominated parts of Africa but has also seen great success in Latin America and the Middle East.

Tom also serves on the board of governors for MAP International, a nonprofit organization that procures, at no or very low cost, medical supplies from U.S. manufacturers for delivery to the poorest of the poor around the world. He has also used his talents and experiences to serve on boards of other nonprofits, including Jeremiah's Promise, a ministry to help foster children. He is an active member and elder in the Presbyterian Church that he and his wife, Kipp, attend, and serves on the leadership committee for the Silicon Valley Prayer Breakfast.

The Root of Tom's Passion

Tom's passion for helping those in need comes from his Christian faith. Church was part of his life from an early age but did not become transformational for him until later in life. In October 1961, he was in the Army during the Cuban military crisis. When his outfit went on alert for a possible confrontation with the Soviets, he turned to God in a much deeper way. "For the first time, I had to get my arms around the questions 'Who is God?', 'What is He expecting of me?', and 'What is my commitment?'"

It was not until the early 1970s when volunteering at a prison in Missouri, however, that God become real to him. "I observed the changed lives of prisoners when they heard the Word of God and saw miracles in their lives resulting from prayer. God spoke to me to say that we all are the same—whether poor or rich, prisoner or free, and He loves each one of us. At that point, the truth of the Bible leaped off the page. I was transformed."

Faith became a guide and lifestyle for Tom. Business in fast-paced Silicon Valley is tough. Decisions often require quick action. The ramifications of choices are often not clear, and the ethical implications are gray. Tom falls back on his faith in those situations. "I frame all my decisions around seeking's God's will," he says. "In business you deal with challenging situations every day, but the tension goes away when you have a relationship with Christ. It gives me a quiet confidence. I do not primarily seek out approval of others, only of God." In making decisions, Tom seeks God's guidance through two filters. "First, would I be comfortable if the decision appeared on the front page of the *New York Times* and second, would I be comfortable if my trusted Christian brothers and sisters were aware of my decision."

Tom Gutshall answered God's call to make a difference in people's lives through his business, nonprofit, and community activities. God's call to serve also led Dave Evans to a successful high-tech career and work as an instructor at Stanford, helping students discern their calling.

Dave Evans

Dave Evans is best known as the co-founder of Electronics Arts, the highly successful interactive software and game company. He believes that his greatest contribution, however, will not come from his high-tech work, but from helping young people find meaning and purpose. Currently, Evans teaches a popular course at Stanford called *Design Your Life*.

Four Careers

Dave has had four careers. His first career was an utterly failed attempt at using his Master's degree in thermosciences to solve the energy crisis back in the mid-70s. While the problem was huge, the world wasn't yet interested in solving it with advanced technologies. Dave says it was his first lesson in the practicality of understanding market readiness.

His second career was as an innovative operating executive in high tech. He worked on the first mouse project He worked on the first mouse project with Apple Computer in the early 1980s, then joined Apple colleague, Trip Hawkins, to start Electronic Arts in 1982. In the late 1980s, he worked on the first voice mail product with VMX in San Jose, which was eventually acquired by Octel/Avaya.

In his third career, beginning in 1990, Dave worked as an independent consultant, helping venture-backed companies manage rapid growth and helping larger companies refine and execute their sales and marketing strategies. One of his motivations in forming a consulting business was to have more time to spend with his young children. His flexible schedule allowed him to coach youth sports and teach Sunday School.

His fourth and current career is as an educator. Dave worked first at the University of California, Berkeley from 2000 through 2008 and now is at Stanford. Although Dave appears to have had four distinctly different careers, there is a theme that connects them. "The real backbone throughout my career has been trying to figure out how to integrate my faith in work." He received little help on faith and work from his local church and Christian friends. "It was infuriating. I was actually sort of mad at Christendom because no one could help me. Then a friend of mine told me about a guy from Colorado who had a clue about it. His name was Gene Thomas, and he developed a theology of work. We spent a weekend learning from Gene. He told us everything he knew about what God says about the integration of faith and work. And our eyes were opened."

As an educator, Dave's mission is to help others find and pursue their purpose and to answer this question: "What should I do with my life and why?"

A Call to Teach

Dave got started in his teaching career following the death of his mother in 2000. Her death forced him to reevaluate his career. He started talking with people doing interesting things and ran into a friend who suggested that he join him to teach at UC Berkeley. Although he didn't have a PhD and didn't have a curriculum, it sounded like a great idea to Dave. He and his friend developed a course called, *How to Find Your Vocation: Is Your Calling, Calling?* "I found a way to teach the Christian doctrine of vocational discernment—the discovery of what God wants us to do with our lives—in a secular setting."

Dave taught at Berkeley for eight years before going to Stanford to teach in the Design Program—a joint effort between the departments of Mechanical Engineering and The School of Art. With a B.S. in mechanical engineering from Stanford and an M.S. in thermosciences, he had a good understanding of design. He proceeded to re-purpose the course he had taught at Berkeley with the help of Bill

Burnett, the Executive Director of the Stanford Design Program. "We reinvented the course through the lens of design thinking and design methodology. That turned out to be a brilliant fit. It started with just a small seminar specifically for design students called *The Designer's Voice*, and grew organically from there."

Designing Your Life

The course was a big hit. When people in the career center heard about what Dave and Bill were doing, they wanted to open it to all students. The *Design Your Life* course they developed is now open to all Stanford juniors and seniors and is a huge success. Each semester the course is oversubscribed. Over 200 students take the course each year. "*Design Your Life* has had a visible cultural effect on the search for vocational identity conversation on campus," says Dave.

What is unique about *Design Your Life* is that it uses engineering methodology and applies it to vocational discernment. Although the course contains no explicit Christian doctrine, Dave states, "A Christian student will find the course to be fully complementary to his or her faith."

Dave runs the class with the simple standing rule that everyone must give honest answers in class. This allows him to be open about his personal Christian faith in answering questions in class and with students during office visits.

While Dave teaches about vocational discernment, it is clear that he has found his calling as well. "Culturally there are three large mentoring infrastructures—the church, the marketplace, and education. I have been active in all three. The reason I am now in education is because that is where the biggest opportunity presented itself. I hope I can contribute to the cultural understanding of what it means to be a young adult and to nurture young people into adulthood in a coherent, thoughtful, and integrated way."

Dave offers advice for young followers of Christ who cannot take his class, but want to determine their calling:

1. **Learn to Pray:** Once you've figured out that life is not simple, and God's will is not one exclusive detailed set of instructions, then it becomes clear that discernment is the critical spiritual faculty one needs to grow. Step one to becoming a discerning person is to develop a real prayer life. A genuine prayer life takes a great deal of investment and incorporates multiple forms of prayer. Surprisingly few Christians pray much or in more than one or two ways. The listening side of the conversation with God is the most important.
2. **Frame the Big Ideas Big:** People rarely think outside their own box, despite the frequency with which we claim to be "out of the box." So, it's important to frame as large and richly textured a box as you can, especially concerning the big ideas. "What is God like?" "What is the nature of what God wants from

us?" "What is meant by God's will?" "Why are we here in the first place?" Then consider what is enough in terms of money, impact, and happiness.

3. **Get the Story:** Our number one counsel to our students is to develop the habit of informational interviewing—which just means talking to people about what they do, why they do it, and how their journey brought them to their current situation. It is important to understand that this type of conversation is decidedly not interviewing for a job. It is a decision-free environment where the goal is to learn about the other person's story. Getting lots of stories is by far the best way to build a base of understanding and insight for your discernment process. If you bring no real-world information, especially the personally authentic stories of people into your prayers, then you leave the Holy Spirit very little to work with in terms of guidance.
4. **Do Stuff:** Life is iterative and takes lots of steps. You're not going to figure it all out up front. Accept that at any moment you are in the midst of a current project that will include lessons, mistakes, compromises, and outcomes from which you'll move to the next thing. Realize that what's going to be happening five years from now is literally unimaginable because you haven't yet met the people or had the experiences or even discovered the issues that will be the organizing platform of that future life. So make the best decisions you can. Show up, do

great work, and be attentive and teachable. Repeat that cycle for the next 50 years.

5. **Pay Attention:** Change is inevitable; growth is optional. Pay attention to what God is growing you into. It never ends. As it says in Philippians 1:6, "... God, who began the good work within you, will continue his work until it is finally finished on the day when Christ Jesus returns." That is the good news! It is the human adventure to which God called us. We are called to continue to grow—to engage God, to understand Him better, to understand ourselves better, and to engage others.

> **Matthew 23:11-12**
>
> "The greatest among you will be your servant. For those who exalt themselves will be humbled, and those who humble themselves will be exalted."

God calls his people to serve; that is, to make a difference. Jesus expects his people to serve others in their families, work, church, and community. Servant-leadership is a popular notion heard not only in the Christian community but in business generally. In business, however, servant leadership is a strategy by which people anticipate something in return—more productive employees, better customer retention, and higher profits. It is simply a wise investment.

To the follower of Christ, however, being a servant is not a strategy to receive a greater gain; it is an *identity* with no return expected, except the joy that comes from obeying

Christ.[2] Ken Yeung, Tom Gutshall, and Dave Evans offer examples of people in different circumstances, with different gifts who were called to live out their faith by serving and making a difference in the lives of others.

Servanthood

To the follower of Christ, being a servant is not a strategy to receive greater gain; it is an identity…

Chapter 15
Concluding Thoughts

I hope you have enjoyed reading the spiritual journeys presented in this book. Although each person's story is unique, their journeys have a common theme. They all found God—some through success, some through adversity, and others by investigating the evidence for faith. And each person answered God's call to become His disciple and to pursue a vocation to fulfill God's purpose for their lives.

The book focuses on successful leaders. Here's why.

Successful people often have the hardest time finding God. Their pursuit of success leaves little room for God. There are deadlines to meet, customers to satisfy, competitors to beat, and families that need attention. At the same time, the satisfaction and rewards that come from achieving success often make finding God difficult—success inflates the ego and reinforces self-reliance rather than reliance on God.

But the leaders profiled in this book did find God. And they found Him in a unique place—Silicon Valley—which makes their journeys of faith even more remarkable. The region's orientation is secular. Faith is counter-cultural. The business focus is on high technology, a fast-paced and competitive industry that attracts ambitious, highly educated people who, in general, are comfortable with themselves, confident, and capable. And the area is blessed with great weather that makes for easy living. Why would leaders in Silicon Valley need God when they seem to have everything—money, prestige, success, and a comfortable lifestyle?

But do they have everything?

Life in Silicon Valley is in many ways no different than life in other places. It is a struggle. People lose jobs and experience adversity and tragedy. Life is busy. Divorce rates are high and many families break up. Like people everywhere, those in Silicon Valley search for meaning and purpose.

The leaders portrayed in this book navigated some of the many obstacles people have to faith in Christ—struggle, the death of a loved one, skepticism, opposing intellectual arguments, and the trappings of success.

But did they really find God. Or did God find them?

The God of the Bible actively pursues everyone. God loves everyone and wants everyone to be saved.[1] God is present and available. But we have to be open to listen to His calling.

Unfortunately, many people are not open. They allow the busyness of life to get in the way. There is little time for God. Others have been hurt by the church and are turned off by what appears to be the hypocritical behavior of Christians.

What about you?

On the chance that the Bible is true, and if you do not yet know Christ as your Savior, why not take the time to find out more about Jesus and who He says He is? Doing so could dramatically transform your life and where you spend eternity. To learn the truth of faith in Christ, let me encourage you to focus less on Christians and more on Jesus.

Faith is volitional. It is a choice. God purposely made it that way. He gave us free will to choose or reject Him. God wants us to love Him but wants our love for Him to be our choice, not His. He plants the desire for Him in us. We simply have to respond. When you think about it, what is a more important decision in life than where to put our faith and trust? The bottom line question is: Do we trust in ourselves, in our work, in our family, or in God?

Understanding how other people have come to faith—in this case, Silicon Valley leaders—is an important step to take. I suggest that you take additional steps. Examine the evidence. Is the Bible true? Is Jesus the Son of God? Did Christ conquer death? Consider reading books that explore the evidence for faith. The Resources section in the back of this book offers recommendations.

To help in your spiritual journey, I developed the *Finding God in Silicon Valley-Interactive Study Guide and Workbook* that can be used in a small group setting to explore issues of faith. In addition, I have a blog that contains additional inspirational stories not in this book and lists other resources. Please see www.FindingGodInSiliconValley.com.

More importantly, start reading the Bible with a sincere desire that God will reveal Himself to you. I suggest that you begin with the New Testament, perhaps the book of John or Matthew. Pray that with God's help your understanding of faith will grow. Start attending church.

Find a church that believes and preaches the Bible (not all do), and join a small group where you can ask questions about the Bible. Often it is in a small group setting that spiritual formation takes place.

Your journey of faith is worth taking.

You will have questions and doubts along the way. Doubt is okay, especially if it leads to further investigation. Faith is not drudgery, as I once thought it. Faith brings joy and contentment. With faith, the burdens of the world, whatever they may be, including the relentless pursuit of success, adversity, and insecurity, are lifted off our backs and shared by Jesus.

The Book of Mathew sums it up best, quoting Jesus: "Come to me, all you who are weary and burdened, and I will give you rest. Take my yoke upon you and learn from me, for I am gentle and humble in heart, and you will find rest for your souls. For my yoke is easy and my burden is light."[2]

Thank you for reading this book. Welcome to a life-long learning and growing experience as you discover who God is and what He has designed for your life.

Index

***** Index items in bold refer to location of text in side boxes.**

C

D

E

H

I

J

K

L

M

N

O

P

R

S

T

U

V

W

Y

Z

Acknowledgements

I have learned in my career that it takes a team of people to complete any project successfully. That is certainly true for *Finding God in Silicon Valley*. I am indebted to many for advice, encouragement, prayers, and their help in reading and editing the manuscript.

First I want to thank the twenty-six people who allowed me to write the stories of their spiritual journeys in this book. Not everyone I asked was comfortable with having their stories published in the public domain. I am indebted to those who did agree to do so, and the many more who allowed me to publish their stories on my blog, *Finding God in Silicon Valley*. It speaks to their character, the depth of their faith, and their desire to help others in their faith journeys.

I want to thank Tom Rees and his staff members, Laura and Mickey, for generously offering their conference room for interviews and various meetings associated with the book.

I owe a special thanks to my wife, Jackie. She was a continual source of encouragement, especially during those times when I felt overwhelmed by the demands of writing the book and fulfilling my many other obligations and responsibilities. Jackie also had the difficult task of reading my early and subsequent chapter drafts, as did my daughter

Christina. Thank you, Jackie and Christina, for your many comments and editing suggestions. Christina also provided help and guidance with a social media strategy. In addition, I want to thank my daughter, Julia, for her help with research on various topics and her overall encouragement and prayers.

Through the years, I have been blessed with having many spiritual mentors. My pastors, Kent Meads, Mike Clark, and Hurmon Hamilton particularly stand out for the many biblically-based messages that helped give me an understanding of the Bible and what it means to be a follower of Christ.

For over twenty years, I have been privileged to participate in a small group of godly men—Phil Ahlfeldt, Erwin Frech, Tom Gutshall, Bruce Hansen, Duane Roberts, and Reid Rutherford. We meet every Friday morning at 6:30 to study, pray, and mentor each other. I know that without them, I would not have grown to understand what it means to practice my faith in work, family, community, and church. This wonderful group of men also provided valuable comments on drafts of *Finding God in Silicon Valley* and the *Finding God in Silicon Valley-Interactive Study Guide and Workbook*. In particular, I want to thank Tom, Reid, and Phil, who work with me on the Silicon Valley Prayer Breakfast, from which I met some of the people profiled in this book. Reid also offered significant personal time helping with my blog and book.

I am also thankful for the prayers and encouragement of those in my Thursday evening church small group—Pat and

Steven Lam, Sehin Belew, Jeannine and Bruce Trott, Lollie Dennis, Kim Tran-Panepucci, Rosemary Preissler, Mona Lei, Ed Soria, and Tony Waller—and my Wednesday morning group—Clif Davidson, Hurmon Hamilton, Dan Monroe, Joe Tan, Tom Klope, Tom Recine, and Bill Clauson. And I owe tremendous gratitude to the Silicon Valley Prayer Breakfast committee for their prayers and support of our mission to reach people for Christ.

I want to thank Jim Ellick, with whom I volunteered in an outreach ministry for several years, and Glenn Moecklemann, both of whom gave me theological clarification when I asked. Glenn was also an enormous help with the technical aspects of my blog.

As with any project of significance, one wants to get the perspective of several people. I am thankful to those who read various versions of the manuscript and offered their valuable insight—Susanna Aughtmon, Charlie Scott, Kelly Monroe-Kullberg, Lil Vaccarello, and Shannon Robinson.

My blog is intimately tied to the writing of the book. Several people were instrumental, and continue to be in developing and enhancing the blog. Pastor and author, John Ortberg, was the first person I interviewed for this project. I want to thank him for encouraging me to first make it a blog before diving into the book. That was good advice.

Regarding the blog, I want to particularly thank web designer and artist Naphy Joiner of Scatter Joy Designs for design and technical help. Naphy also took the photograph on the book cover. Brandon Elder also offered help as I have encountered technical challenges. Andy Wong provided encouragement and help with social media.

I owe much gratitude to Glen Aubrey of Creative Team Publishing and his staff for tirelessly helping with the many tasks needed to complete the writing and editing of the book and study guide, and getting it to market. Glen was a big source of enthusiasm, encouragement, and suggestions. Thank you, Major General and author, Bob Dees, for suggesting Glen to me.

I want to thank Justin Aubrey for the cover design, and Al Clark for his photograph of me for the cover.

Publicist Scott Spiewak provided enormous help lining up interviews with national news outlets and several publications. In the process, Scott has become a good friend. I want to thank high-tech businessman and author Steven Richards for suggesting Scott to me and for his encouragement.

I have also had the good fortune to have many friends and family members who embraced my project and provided their support—Diane and David Richardson, Janet Gustafson, Rick Vaccarello, Daniel Richardson, Matt Scott, Tom and Michele Spengler, Manuel and Susan Monteiro, Chuck and Alice McCormack, Jon and Mary Gorham, John and Deborah Baldwin, Tim and Leslie Maier, Dave Chae, Ryan Derfler, and longtime business partner, Steve Randesi and his wife Diane, among others.

Finally, I want to thank my Savior, Jesus Christ, for accepting me as His child, for never forsaking me when I rebelled, and from whom I get my inspiration.

Products and Services

Finding God in Silicon Valley: Spiritual Journeys in a High-Tech World—for quantity orders (over 25 books), please email: info@springstoneco.com

Finding God in Silicon Valley-Interactive Study Guide and Workbook—a great resource for small group discussions. Order at www.FindingGodInSiliconValley.com

Skip Vaccarello is available as a speaker, business mentor, and consultant. Email: skip@findinggodsv.com

Additional resources and stories like those you read in *Finding God in Silicon Valley* are available at: www.FindingGodInSiliconValley.com

Resources

Books Written by People Profiled in *Finding God in Silicon Valley: Spiritual Journeys in a High-Tech World*

All the Evidence You Will Ever Need: A Scientist Believes in the Gospel of Jesus Christ by Dr. Paul Baba

Ready, Fire, Aim by Paul Ely

The Juggling Act: Bringing Balance to Faith, Family, and Work by Pat Gelsinger

Books I have Found Helpful in My Faith Journey

Spiritual Journeys

Finding God at Harvard: Spiritual Journeys of Thinking Christians by Kelly Monroe (Kullberg)

Born Again by Charles Colson

Classic and Current Books on What it Means to be a Christian

Basic Christianity by John Stott

Experiencing God: Knowing and Doing the Will of God by Henry Blackaby

Knowing God by J.J. Packer

Mere Christianity by C.S. Lewis

The Knowledge of the Holy by A.W. Tozer

The Purpose Driven Life by Rick Warren

Daily Devotionals

As the Spirit Moves by Stephen Chapin Garner

My Utmost for His Highest by Oswald Chambers

Thoughts from the Diary of a Desperate Man by Walter A. Henrichsen (This book is not available new, but might be found used.)

Books on Death, Heaven, Hell, and Immortality

Beyond Death: Exploring the Evidence for Immortality
by Gary Habermas and J. P. Moreland

Erasing Hell by Francis Chan

Heaven by Randy Alcorn

Heaven is for Real: A Little Boy's Astounding Story of His Trip to Heaven and Back
by Todd Burpo and Lynn Vincent

Books on Faith and Work

Anointed for Business by Ed Silvoso

Believers in Business by Laura Nash

God at Work by Rick Marshall

Jesus CEO: Using Ancient Wisdom for Visionary Leaderships
by Laurie Beth Jones

Loving Monday by John Beckett

Transforming the Workplace for Christ by William Nix

Why Business Matters to God by Jeff Van Duzer

Books on Living the Christian Life

Celebration of Discipline: The Path to Spiritual Growth by Richard J. Foster

Crazy Love: Overwhelmed by a Relentless God by Francis Chan

Face to Face with God by Bill Johnson

Forgotten God: Reversing our Tragic Neglect of the Holy Spirit by Francis Chan

The Life You Always Wanted by John Ortberg

The Me I Want to Become: Becoming God's Best Version of You by John Ortberg

How Now Shall We Live? by Charles Colson and Nancy Pearcy

Radical: Taking Back Your Faith from the American Dream by David Platt

The Spirit of the Disciplines: Understanding How God Changes Lives by Dallas Willard

If You Want to Walk on the Water, You've Got to Get Out of the Boat by John Ortberg

What so Amazing about Grace? by Phillip Yancey

Books on Faith and Science, Creation and Darwinism

Darwin on Trial by Phillip Johnson

Genesis and the Big Bang by Gerald L. Schroeder

Science and Christianity: Conflict or Coherence by Henry Schaefer

Science Speaks, Scientific Proof of the Accuracy of Prophecy and the Bible by Peter W. Stoner M.S. and Robert C. Newman S.T.M. PhD

Science Speaks by Peter W. Stoner—online edition

The Language of God: A Scientist Presents Evidence for Belief by Francis Collins

Books on Comparative Religions
(Christian perspective)

Many Gods Many Lords by Daniel Clendenin

Relativism: Feet Firmly Planted in Mid-Air by Francis Beckwith and Gregory Koukl

So What's the Difference by Fritz Ridenour

Books on Christian Apologetics

Answers to Tough Questions Skeptics Ask About the Christian Faith by Josh McDowell and Don Stewart

Baker Encyclopedia of Christian Apologetics by Norman L. Geisler

Christian Apologetics by Norman L. Geisler

Night with a Perfect Stranger: The Conversation which Changes Everything by David Gregory

Eternity in the Hearts: Startling Evidence of Belief in the One True God in Hundreds of Cultures Throughout the World by Don Richardson

I'm Glad You've Asked by Ken Boa and Larry Moody

Know What You Believe by Paul E. Little

Letters from a Skeptic: A Son Wrestles with His Father's Questions about Christianity by Gregory A. Boyd and Edward K. Boyd

Mere Christianity by C.S. Lewis

More than a Carpenter by Josh McDowell

The Case for Christ by Lee Strobel

The Case for Christianity by C.S. Lewis

The Case for Easter by Lee Strobel

The Case for Faith by Lee Strobel

The Historical Jesus by Gary Habermas

The New Evidence that Demands a Verdict by Josh McDowell

The Question of God – C.S. Lewis and Sigmund Freud Debate God, Sex, Love, and the Meaning of Life by Dr. Armand M. Nicholi

The Reason for God in the Age of Skepticism by Timothy Keller

The Resurrection Factor by Josh McDowell
Who is this Man? by John Ortberg

Understanding the Trinity by Alister E. McGrath

Citations

God and Silicon Valley:
The Journey Begins

1. http://www.goodreads.com/quotes/4140
2. With high tech companies and workers expanding across the San Francisco Area, I use the terms Silicon Valley and the Bay Area interchangeably when talking about the region, but generally use the term Silicon Valley when discussing technology related subjects.
3. "Reid Hoffman, Mr. LinkedIn," *FT Magazine*, March 17, 2012 -- http://www.ft.com/cms/s/2/df0f609c-6e31-11e1-baa5-00144feab49a.html#axzz38Jd2mePx
4. "Startup Hubs Around the World: Silicon Valley," *Entrepreneurial Insights*" blog, June 28, 2014 -- http://www.entrepreneurial-insights.com/startup-hubs-around-world-silicon-valley/
5. United States Census Bureau, 2010.
6. *Caldwell Banker Home Listing Report* 2014 -- http://blog.coldwellbanker.com/hlr-2014/
7. *Barna Reports – Cities* "San Francisco-Oakland-San Jose: A Profile of Residents in the Greater San Francisco-Oakland-San Jose Area"
8. "In the U.S., 77% Identify as Christian" by Frank Newport, Gallop, December 24, 2012 -- http://www.gallup.com/poll/159548/identify-christian.aspx
9. A basic biblical concept is that people are saved by God's grace, not by what they do – sometimes referred to as "works," A key Bible verse that describes this is Ephesians 2:8-9, "For it is by grace you have been saved, through faith and this is not from yourselves, it is a gift from God not by works, so that no one can boast."

Section One: Faith and Success

1. From author's interview with Paul Ely

Chapter 1

Gratitude: Discovering God's Impact on Our Lives

1. http://www.whatchristianswanttoknow.com/21-inspirational-a-w-tozer-quotes/
2. NetValley, October 31, 2010. A summary of a talk by Carolyn Tajnai, Director of the Stanford Computer Forum and Assistant Chairman in Stanford's Department of Computer Science
3. SV 150: Searchable database of Silicon Valley's top 150 companies for 2014, by Daniel Willis and Jack Davis, Bay Area News Group
4. Paul Ely, *Ready, Fire, Aim*, page 66
5. Paul Ely, *Ready, Fire, Aim*, page 102
6. Paul Ely, *Ready, Fire, Aim*, page 130
7. James 1:17
8. Paul Ely, *Ready, Fire, Aim*, page 131
9. Paul Ely, *Ready, Fire, Aim*, page 132
10. Paul Ely, *Ready, Fire, Aim*, page 134
11. John 16:7"But very truly I tell you, it is for your good that I am going away. Unless I go away, the Advocate will not come to you; but if I go, I will send him to you." (NIV) Other translations use the word Helper, Comforter, Counselor, and Encourager—all widely recognized by scholars to mean the Holy Spirit.

Chapter 2

Success and Surrender

1. C.S. Lewis, *Mere Christianity*, HarporOne, Copyright 1952 and 1980, C.S. Lewis Pte. Ltd., page 196.
2. *Consumer Reports* July 2013 – Online: http://www.consumerreports.org/content/dam/cro/magazine-articles/2013/September/CR-SEPT13-p34-Surgery-Common-Rate-Branded.pdf
3. 1Timothy 6:9, 10

4. Oswald Chambers, edited by James Reiman, *My Utmost for His Highest*, Discovery House Publishers, 1992, page January 1
5. Rick Warren, *The Purpose Driven Life*, Zondervan 2002, page 17
6. http://biblicalviewpoint.com/

Chapter 3
Success Redefined

1. Zig Ziglar. BrainyQuote.com, Xplore Inc, 2015, http://www.brainyquote.com/quotes/quotes/z/zigziglar381972.html
2. Pat Gelsinger, *The Juggling Act*, David Cook Publishers, 2008, page 33.
3. Pat Gelsinger, *The Juggling Act*, David Cook Publishers, 2008, page 34.
4. Pat Gelsinger, *The Juggling Act*, David Cook Publishers, 2008, page 41
5. Pat Gelsinger, *The Juggling Act*, David Cook Publishers, 2008, page 42.
6. Comments by Pat Gelsinger at the 2014 Silicon Valley Prayer Breakfast
7. Comments by Pat Gelsinger at the 2014 Silicon Valley Prayer Breakfast

Chapter 4
Hollow Success

1. Ralph Waldo Emerson. BrainyQuote.com, Xplore Inc, 2015. http://www.brainyquote.com/quotes/quotes/r/ralphwaldo103415.html
2. *Harvard Crimson*, October 7, 1976 by John Donley and Gay Seidman
3. Gregg Williams and Rob Moore, interviewers, "The Apple Story," Byte, January 1985, pp 173-4.

Section Two: Reason, Science and Faith

1. Blaise Pascal. BrainyQuote.com, Xplore Inc, 2015. http://www.brainyquote.com/quotes/quotes/b/blaisepasc121377.html

Chapter 5
Faith and Reason

1. Martin Luther King, Jr. BrainyQuote.com, Xplore Inc., 2015. http://www.brainyquote.com/quotes/quotes/m/martinluth105087.html
2. https://en.wikipedia.org/wiki/Opium_of_the_people The book of Isaiah was written approximately 600 to 800 years before Christ. Isaiah 53, which was particularly meaningful to Brent, includes this verse: "Surely he took up our pain and bore our suffering, yet we considered him punished by God, stricken by him, and afflicted. But he was pierced for our transgressions, he was crushed for our iniquities; the punishment that brought us peace was on him, and by his wounds we are healed. We all, like sheep, have gone astray, each of us has turned to our own way; and the Lord has laid on him the iniquity of us all." (Isaiah 53:4-6) The verses appear to prophesize Christ's dying for our sins on the cross.
3. Psalm 22, which is attributed to King David, Israel's second king who lived approximately 1,000 years before Christ, also appear to foretell Christ's crucifixion. Here is a sampling of Psalm 22: "Dogs surround me, a pack of villains encircles me; they pierce my hands and my feet. All my bones are on display; people stare and gloat over me. They divide my clothes among them and cast lots for my garment." (Psalm 22:16-22)
4. Steiner, Joseph, *Science Speaks*, Chapter 3, http://sciencespeaks.dstoner.net/Christ_of_Prophecy.html#c9
5. McDowell, Josh, *The Resurrection Factor*, 1981, is now out of print, and its recent edition, September 2005. Josh McDowell's *The New Evidence that Demands a Verdict* contains similar information.

Chapter 6
Science and Faith

1. Amir D. Azcel, Why Science Does Not Disprove God, Harper Collins (Australia Pty. Ltd.), 2014, page 19

2. Richard Dawkins. BrainyQuote.com, Xplore Inc., 2015.http://www.brainyquote.com/quotes/quotes/r/richarddaw141335.html
3. Amir D. Azcel, *Why Science Does Not Disprove God*, Harper Collins (Australia Pty. Ltd., 2014, page 5
4. Henry B. Schaeffer, *Science and Christianity: Conflict or Coherence?*, University of Georgia, 2008.
5. Francis S. Collins, *The Language of God: A Scientist Presents Evidence for Belief*, Free Press, a division of Simon and Schuster, Inc., 2006
6. Francis S. Collins, *The Language of God: A Scientist Presents Evidence for Belief*, Free Press, a division of Simon and Schuster, Inc., 2006, Introduction.
7. Paul Baba, *All the Evidence You will Ever Need: A Scientist Believes in the Gospel of Jesus Christ*, Wipf and Stock Publishers, 2008, page 147.
8. In 1 Corinthians 15:13, 14, the Apostle Paul says: For if there is no resurrection of the dead, then Christ has not been raised either. And if Christ has not been raised, then all our preaching is useless, and your faith is useless.

Chapter 7
The Search for Truth

1. Blaise Pascal, *Pensees*, 1670, Section II, No. 72
2. John 18:37. Jesus makes this statement when Pontius Pilot asks Jesus if He is the King of the Jews. Pilot replies "What is truth?"
3. John 8:31, 32. Jesus made these comments when people were disputing who Jesus was. He addressed these remarks to the Jews who believed in Him.
4. William Hurlbut, "Evolutionary Theory and the Emergence of Moral Nature", *Journal of Psychology and Theology*, December 22, 2001.
5. William Hurlbut, "Evolutionary Theory and the Emergence of Moral Nature", *Journal of Psychology and Theology*, December 22, 2001.

6. William Hurlbut, "Evolutionary Theory and the Emergence of Moral Nature", *Journal of Psychology and Theology*, December 22, 2001.
7. William Hurlbut, "Evolutionary Theory and the Emergence of Moral Nature", *Journal of Psychology and Theology*, December 22, 2001.
8. William Hurlbut, "Evolutionary Theory and the Emergence of Moral Nature", *Journal of Psychology and Theology*, December 22, 2001.
9. Matthew 6:33 and quoted in William Hurlbut, "Evolutionary Theory and the Emergence of Moral Nature", *Journal of Psychology and Theology*, December 22, 2001.
10. William Hurlbut, "Evolutionary Theory and the Emergence of Moral Nature", *Journal of Psychology and Theology*, December 22, 2001.
11. William Hurlbut, "Evolutionary Theory and the Emergence of Moral Nature", *Journal of Psychology and Theology*, December 22, 2001.
12. William, B. Hurlbut, "St. Francis. Christian Love, and the Biotechnical Future", *The New Atlantis: A Journal of Technology & Society*, www.TheNewAtlantis.com.
13. William, B. Hurlbut, "St. Francis. Christian Love, and the Biotechnical Future", *The New Atlantis: A Journal of Technology & Society*, www.TheNewAtlantis.com.
14. William, B. Hurlbut, "St. Francis. Christian Love, and the Biotechnical Future", *The New Atlantis: A Journal of Technology & Society*, www.TheNewAtlantis.com.
15. William, B. Hurlbut, "St. Francis. Christian Love, and the Biotechnical Future", *The New Atlantis: A Journal of Technology & Society*, www.TheNewAtlantis.com.
16. A March 6, 2015 talk at the Mayo Clinic in Rochester Minnesota by Dr. William Hurlbut titled: "Professional or Provider: Biotechnology, Suffering, and Human Aspiration."

17. A March 6, 2015 talk at the Mayo Clinic in Rochester Minnesota by Dr. William Hurlbut titled: "Professional or Provider: Biotechnology, Suffering, and Human Aspiration."
18. A March 6, 2015 talk at the Mayo Clinic in Rochester Minnesota by Dr. William Hurlbut titled: "Professional or Provider: Biotechnology, Suffering, and Human Aspiration."
19. A March 6, 2015 talk at the Mayo Clinic in Rochester Minnesota by Dr. William Hurlbut titled: "Professional or Provider: Biotechnology, Suffering, and Human Aspiration."
20. A March 6, 2015 talk at the Mayo Clinic in Rochester Minnesota by Dr. William Hurlbut titled: "Professional or Provider: Biotechnology, Suffering, and Human Aspiration."
21. A talk by William B. Hurlbut, "Rewiring the Brain: the Uses and Abuses of Neurotechnology" at a Stanford Alumni gathering in November, 2014.

Section Three: Struggle, Pain, and Faith

1. C.S. Lewis, *The Problem of Pain*, HarperCollins, 1940/1996, page 91.
2. 1 Peter 4:12 "Dear friends, do not be surprised at the fiery ordeal that has come on you to test you, as though something strange were happening to you."
3. Romans 5:3-4 "… we also glory in our sufferings, because we know that suffering produces perseverance; [4]perseverance, character; and character, hope.
4. Romans 8:28 "And we know that in all things God works for the good of those who love him, who have been called according to his purpose."

Chapter 8

Peace in the Face of Adversity

1. http://www.vincelombardi.com/quotes.html, Family of Vince Lombardi c/o Luminary Group LLC.

2. Many books have been written on the biblical concept of pain and suffering. Two I recommend are *The Problem* of Pain by C.S. Lewis and *Walking with God Through Pain* by Timothy Keller.

Chapter 9
Struggle, Prayer, and Healing

1. Mother Teresa, *A Simple Path,* Ballantine Books, 1995, page 8
2. Isaiah 55:8-9 makes the point that we do not always know God's plan. "'For my thoughts are not your thoughts, neither are your ways my ways,' declares the Lord, 'As the heavens are higher than the earth, so my ways are higher than your ways and my thoughts are higher than your thoughts.'"
3. Acts 2 describes the miracle of the coming of the Holy Spirit to the discibles. The key verses are 2:1-4: "When the day of Pentecost came, they were all together in one place. Suddenly a sound like the blowing of a violent wind came from heaven and filled the whole house where they were sitting. They saw what seemed to be tongues of fire that separated and came to rest on each of them. All of them were filled with the Holy Spirit and began to speak in other tongues as the Spirit enabled them."
4. Romans 8:3-5
5. Romans 8:28

Chapter 10
Pain and Purpose

1. Rick Warren, *The Purpose Driven Life*, Zondervan, 2002, page 196
2. David Batstone, *Not for Sale*, HarperCollins, 2010
3. Malcolm Gladwell, *Tipping Point*, Little Brown and Company, March 2000
4. Isaiah 55: 8-9: "For my thoughts are not your thoughts, neither are your ways my ways, "declares the Lord. "As the heavens are higher than the earth, so are my ways higher than your ways and my thoughts than your thoughts."
5. See Deuteronomy 31:8: "The Lord himself goes before you and will be with you; he will never leave you nor forsake you. Do not

be afraid; do not be discouraged." And 1 Peter 5:7: "Cast all your anxiety on him because he cares for you."

6. The full verse is Romans 12:2: "Do not conform to the pattern of this world, but be transformed by the renewing of your mind. Then you will be able to test and approve what God's will is—his good, pleasing and perfect will."
7. *Inside the Vatican*, January, 2014.

Section Four: A Higher Calling

1. Oswald Chambers, edited by James Reiman, *My Utmost for His Highest*, Discovery House Publishers, 1992, January 16.
2. Abram was called by God to become the leader not only of the Jews, but also of all nations and people. Genesis 12:1-3 reads: The Lord had said to Abram, "Go from your country, your people and your father's household to the land I will show you. "I will make you into a great nation, and I will bless you; I will make your name great, and you will be a blessing. I will bless those who bless you, and whoever curses you I will curse; and all peoples on earth will be blessed through you."
3. Genesis 17:5
4. Exodus 3
5. Matthew 4:18-20
6. Mathew 9:9
7. John 15:12-15. In this passage, Jesus helps define what he means by friend—someone who lays down his life for another, as Jesus did for us. He also calls his disciples to obedience. "My command is this: Love each other as I have loved you. Greater love has no one than this: to lay down one's life for one's friends. You are my friends if you do what I command. I no longer call you servants, because a servant does not know his master's business. Instead, I have called you friends, for everything that I learned from my Father I have made known to you."

Chapter 11

Following God's Call

1. Mark Labberton, *Called,* IVP Books 2014, page 135
2. Luke 10:1-23
3. 2 Thessalonians 3:10: "For even when we were with you, we gave you this rule: 'The one who is unwilling to work shall not eat."'

Chapter 12

Business as a Calling

1. Ken Eldred, *God is at Work: Transforming People and Nations Through Business*, Regal Books, 2005, page 68
2. The Parable of the Talents can be found in Matthew 25:14-30 and Luke 19:12-27.
3. http://www.goodreads.com/quotes/22155-i-like-your-christ-i-do-not-like-your-christians. Note: Gandhi is often quoted as saying this, but whether he said it is questionable. It does make the point that people are often turned off by the apparent hypocrisy of Christians. The Bible makes the same point—for God's followers to show their faith by their behavior. For example, James 1:22 reads: "Do not merely listen to the word, and so deceive yourselves. Do what it says."
4. Matthew 18:15 reads: "If your brother or sister sins, go and point out their fault, just between the two of you. If they listen to you, you have won them over."
5. Frederick Buechner, *Wishful Thinking: A Theological ABC,* New York Harper One, 1994
   http://www.goodreads.com/quotes/140448-the-place-god-calls-you-to-is-the-place-where

Chapter 13

Called as an Entrepreneur

1. Peter Drucker. BrainyQuote.com, Xplore Inc, 2015, http://www.brainyquote.com/quotes/quotes/p/peterdruck154441.html

2. Pharisees were a Jewish sect that Jesus often criticized for their hypocrisy and legalistic approach to faith.
3. Matthew 5:14-15: "You are the light of the world. A town built on a hill cannot be hidden. Neither do people light a lamp and put it under a bowl. Instead they put it on its stand, and it gives light to everyone in the house. In the same way, let your light shine before others, that they may see your good deeds and glorify your Father in heaven."

Chapter 14
Called to Serve

1. In a sermon by Dr. Martin Luther King on February 4, 1968 at the Ebenezer Baptist Church in Atlanta. Found at: http://www.karmatube.org/videos.php?id=2959
2. The "Parable of the Talents" as recorded in Matthew 25:14-29 is an example of what it means to serve. The master in the parable said to his servants who wisely invested the talents "Well done, good and faithful servant." These are the words the faithful follower of Christ hopes to hear from Jesus when he sees Him face to face.

Chapter 15
Concluding Thoughts

1. God wants everyone to know Him and to be their Savior. Several Bible verses reflect this theme. Here are three:
    a. John 3:17 – "God sent his Son into the world not to judge the world, but to save the world through him."
    b. Titus 2:11 – "For the grace of God has been revealed, bringing salvation to all people."
    c. 1 Timothy 2:3-5 – "...God our Savior, who desires all men to be saved and to come to the knowledge of the truth. For there is one God, and one mediator also between God and men, the man Christ Jesus,..."
2. Matthew 11:28-30

CPSIA information can be obtained at www.ICGtesting.com
Printed in the USA
LVOW07s1334291015

460287LV00003B/191/P

9 780996 371926